Stick It to Me, Baby!

Inserting Spirit Into the Science of Infertility

Dr. Danica Thornberry, DAOM

with Kuwana Haulsey

BALBOA.PRESS

A DIVISION OF HAY HOUSE

Balboa Press books may be ordered through booksellers or by contacting:

Balboa Press
A Division of Hay House
1663 Liberty Drive
Bloomington, IN 47403
www.balboapress.com
844-682-1282

Because of the dynamic nature of the Internet, any web addresses or links contained in this book may have changed since publication and may no longer be valid. The views expressed in this work are solely those of the author and do not necessarily reflect the views of the publisher, and the publisher hereby disclaims any responsibility for them.

The author of this book does not dispense medical advice or prescribe the use of any technique as a form of treatment for physical, emotional, or medical problems without the advice of a physician, either directly or indirectly. The intent of the author is only to offer information of a general nature to help you in your quest for emotional and spiritual well-being. In the event you use any of the information in this book for yourself, which is your constitutional right, the author and the publisher assume no responsibility for your actions.

Any people depicted in stock imagery provided by Thinkstock are models, and such images are being used for illustrative purposes only.
Certain stock imagery © Thinkstock.

Print information available on the last page.

ISBN: 978-1-5043-5108-9 (sc)
ISBN: 978-1-5043-5109-6 (e)

Library of Congress Control Number: 2016902135

Balboa Press rev. date: 11/11/2022

Praise for *Stick It to Me, Baby!*

"To a masterful understanding and practice of Chinese medicine in treating infertility, Danica reminds us of the wisdom behind the mind-body-spirit connection in creating a fertile, welcoming environment for a healthy baby. This book is sure to give women new hope, and offers a new approach to fertility treatment."

Michael Bernard Beckwith
Author of *Life Visioning*

"Beautiful work. Danica Thornberry has poured forth the most important aspect of Chinese medicine - the healing capacity of one's own heart. It is so easy to get lost in the science; to think that our lab values are indicative of our potential, and to be driven by the fear of letting our heart's desires slip by. Danica captures what I believe to be the heart of Chinese medicine - being rooted in the spirit of one's own truth, and letting it lead the way. Refreshing."

Randine Lewis, L.Ac., Ph.D.
Author of *The Infertility Cure*,
and *The Way of the Fertile Soul*

"Danica has written a compelling, honest and empowering tome on the infertility journey and the opportunity it presents for self- growth and self-healing. Bravo!"

Brenda Strong
National Spokesperson of the American Fertility Association,
Founder of Strong Yoga 4 Women and Award-Winning Actress

"This is a great book to help women through their fertility journey with far less anxiety, more peace, and a better understanding of their body. If you want to be deeply engaged in your fertility journey, this is a wonderful resource and a brilliant guide to help you along the path."

————————

"Danica has cracked the code to women's fertility! *Stick It to Me, Baby!* illustrates how personal and emotional "readiness" for pregnancy can help create an optimal environment for embryo implantation and growth. Using acupuncture, spiritual counseling and dietary changes, Danica is able to redirect a woman's focus and energy to empower them towards conception."

————————

"Danica reframes how we view our fertility – beginning with the concept that our *uterus is our second heart*. She provides an armamentarium for women to become proactive participants in their fertility care."

————————

"*Stick It to Me, Baby!* provides a comprehensive and thought provoking overview into the plight that infertile women face, from a perspective that expands our understanding of Eastern approaches and adds to what we often consider a Western medical problem. Danica adeptly combines her personal life experiences with an unparalleled understanding of Chinese medicine, thereby making difficult concepts easily understood and relatable. As a reproductive psychiatrist who specializes in the treatment of women in all stages of reproductive events, I appreciate how Danica's insights further my appreciation for an East meets West approach in this very exciting and specialized field. *Stick it to Me, Baby!* will bring hope, potential and a brighter future for those who sign up for the incredible journey of bringing new life to the world."

Merrill Sparago, M.D.
Reproductive Psychiatry - Private Practice
Los Angeles, CA

"I've had the honor of seeing Danica's dream of helping women become mothers grow and blossom over many years. She has an innate wisdom that guides her, an intellect that is insatiable, and the kindest heart. In *Stick It to Me, Baby!* she leads with her insightfulness on a mission to help others heal their bodies and souls. I have witnessed several women greatly benefit from her treatment approach. She is truly a pioneer in the field of infertility, utilizing the blended energy of acupuncture and spiritual medicine."

Debi Jenkins Frankle, LMFT
Co-Founder
Calabasas Counseling and Grief Recovery Center

"In *Stick It to Me, Baby!* Danica bravely reveals and interweaves her personal infertility journey into a tapestry of numerous other infertile women's comparative experiences—providing the reader with a compassionate, intense and penetrating view of a women's emotional, physical, and spiritual growth that occurs along their path towards motherhood. Her words will leave you feeling reflective with incredible insight into the hearts of women living through infertility."

Patrisha Taylor, MFT, PhD (c)
Maternal Mental Health Task Force Supervisor

To Kira and Jack Connors

Determined little spirits who came to me despite many odds,
to reveal what is possible when we open up to receive a miracle.

The stories in this book are true to the best of my recollection. However, the names of the women and some details about their lives have been changed to protect their privacy.

Infertility is a growing, non-discriminatory health condition that affects women and men of all races, sexual orientations, and income levels.

"Live your life in such a way that makes people want to read your story."

Author Unknown

Table of Contents

Say YES! to the Process of Becoming a Mother

FOREWORD

by Richard P. Marrs, M.D.

In *Stick It to Me, Baby!* Danica Thornberry has told a story of the successes and failures, triumphs and losses, and the perils and pitfalls of human infertility. Danica has woven into this work her own story of the physical, emotional and spiritual aspects of her personal infertility saga – to give readers an even more first-hand look at the process. Danica's amazing insight into the human spirit and her outstanding abilities with Chinese medicine give the reader a sense of *what is possible* for individuals struggling with the harsh reality of infertility.

Danica uses real life stories of patient cases and reveals the methods she has used to help resolve these patients' conditions. While reading these clinical scenarios the reader will be viewing the clinical situation through Danica's eyes. She takes us through the medical implications, both Western and Eastern alternatives and then, we see the woman's spiritual, emotional transformation; which is never really examined or investigated to a great extent.

Danica has done a masterful job of displaying how important the spiritual/emotional involvement in the treatment of infertility really is. Within each story, an infertile patient's medical and physiological treatment is clearly explained and combined with an appropriately matched holistic treatment to give readers greater perspective.

An exploration of the spiritual basis behind the individual women's diagnoses is clearly demonstrated in Danica's case discussions. I have never seen a better demonstration of how important it is to blend these facets of patient treatment, in order to affect the outcome of therapy.

Stick It to Me, Baby! is a factual, hard hitting, no holds barred tome on the 21st Century approach to fertility treatment. It is not a "feel good" book — but rather it is a *must read* for every person dealing with fertility issues. It is the best preparation for all those individuals who must face the ups and downs of fertility treatment. After reading *Stick It to Me, Baby!* the reader will definitely become an "empowered self-advocate," which is the best way to prepare oneself for this journey ahead.

Richard P. Marrs, M.D.
Internationally recognized leader in IVF, known for successfully creating the first baby in the world from a frozen embryo.

Part 1

Embrace These Basic Concepts

Introduction

The woman sitting before me was thirty-nine-years-old, recently married, and had been desperately trying to get pregnant for six months. She revealed that she couldn't sleep and had terrible headaches. She'd often find herself awake at night, her mind racing and her body soaked in sweat for seemingly no reason. Her moods fluctuated without warning, leaving her by turns snappish, anxious, and tearful. Her doctor recently informed her that, although she wanted to have a baby, she was experiencing peri-menopause.

While listening to this infertility patient recount her symptoms, I was struck by a disconcerting thought: *I have all those symptoms.*

I was only thirty-one at the time. I was single and not the slightest bit interested in having a baby. I had just begun building my new acupuncture practice and was consumed with the task of turning it into a success. I attributed my long list of symptoms to work stress.

Because acupuncture is known for its consistent ability to activate the body's calming hormones (endorphins, oxytocin, and serotonin), it's a modality that blends quite nicely into infertility treatment. Being located in Los Angeles, the hub for many of the world's best fertility centers, I quickly created a very busy practice, with no room in my schedule for a baby.

I chose to specialize in infertility because these patients are the most willing to make drastic changes for a successful outcome. I find such personal transformation exhilarating. It never occurred to me that the reason I enjoyed working with these patients so much was because I was about to be labeled "infertile" myself.

On this specific day, my patient Christine was presenting with an elevated FSH (Follicle Stimulating Hormone) score of 19. Studies at that time, back in 2002, suggested that a high score of this ovarian marker could implicate her ovaries were "failing" and her eggs were likely "too old" to result in a healthy pregnancy. Due to her high FSH score, Christine was excluded from the possibility of starting IVF (In Vitro Fertilization) that month. Her doctor warned that the ovarian stimulation aspect of an IVF protocol could potentially harm her ovaries, throwing her into an immediate menopause. Accordingly, she found her way to acupuncture and asked me to help bring her FSH levels down in hopes that she'd be considered a candidate for IVF in the coming months.

In the middle of telling her story, Christine stopped and said, "Danica, you're young, but if you have *any* of these symptoms, go check your hormone levels. Don't wait until you are my age to find out if you have a problem. It will be too late."

Intrigued, I listened to her advice, and with the onset of my next menstrual period, took myself in for blood work. The lab director, a friend of mine, laughed and said, "Oh, come on, Danica. You're only thirty-one. You're nowhere near menopause."

"I don't know," I replied. "You might be surprised by the results."

My friend called me a few days later. "I am so sorry," he said as he gave me the news.

My FSH score came back elevated at 21, and my estrogen was almost non-existent. My score was higher than any of my infertility patients at the time! My FSH score should have been about 7. This high score meant, like Christine, I wouldn't be an eligible candidate for IVF, and furthermore, my ovaries would always be considered at risk of POF (Premature Ovarian Failure).

Once I received those initial results, I started leaning on my research background and began tracking subsequent FSH scores. I scheduled ultrasounds at different points in my cycle to see if I had properly maturing follicles. To each doctor's surprise, I had very few follicles and they were not ovulating properly.

Soon doctors were telling me I would need another woman's eggs to have a child, based on my blood work and ultrasound images. At first I was surprised. Then I was crushed. A few months full of self-pity passed, then I felt compelled to prove the science wrong.

Though I wasn't trying to get pregnant at the time, the thought of being denied a child someday made my heart sink. So I opted to become the subject of my own "experiment." I decided to look extensively at my ovaries and their role in my body, while examining other areas of my life – figuring my choices may have somehow impacted my ovarian health.

Like most people, I used to regard infertility as a physical problem, a "health condition" to be treated with medicine. I had no idea that a spiritual path was being revealed to me inside my infertile diagnosis; nor did I know that my diagnosis would later be reversed once I committed to a journey of personal discovery and transformation!

The first part of my transformation involved making a very awkward phone call to an ex-boyfriend – not to get back together, but to ask for some vials of sperm, to bank for the future.

"Once I recover my ovaries, I think our genes would mix well," I said matter-of-factly. Surprisingly, he said yes—but with the condition that *together* we would raise any child created from his sperm.

"As a couple?" I asked, shocked. "Given our history, I don't think that's a good idea." Our on-again, off-again relationship of nearly four years had finally led us to be just friends, and I thought that suited us much better.

"If you intend to raise kids alone who are half mine, I won't agree to that. I can't help you, sorry," he said before hanging up. I respected him for setting that boundary with me and set out to begin my self-discovery experiment. I didn't know that five years later, Dan and I would revisit this conversation.

During this five-year interim, I pored over all the information I could find about healing infertility naturally. I changed my diet, began an herbal regimen, and made acupuncture a weekly priority for myself. I went beyond my comfort zone and took a belly dancing class — to get in touch with the "hidden feminine" aspects of myself. I started journaling consistently and took various classes about Chinese gynecology.

Along the way, I dispensed my newfound wisdom to my patients and the other acupuncturists working in my office. My personal enthusiasm for the subject flowed effortlessly inside the treatment rooms. Over 500 live births later, these women, previously labeled "infertile," were consistently beating high odds. It seemed my harrowing personal experience with infertility offered something positive!

By thirty-six, I was feeling noticeably different. Five years had passed since my initiation into the world of ultrasounds, blood tests, and uncomfortable procedures. My FSH score was still too high for IVF and I had no partner, but I somehow felt incredibly healthy and fertile. Working on my personal issues and directing the patients to *their* kids had changed me, and it was definitely for the better.

I watched countless women benefit from my inner exploration. Though I was happy to help them become pregnant, I cried a lot in private moments and often felt sorry for myself. As those years unfolded, I found out that not only was I experiencing premature ovarian failure and early menopause, I also had a blocked fallopian tube and needed a second laparoscopic surgery for severe endometriosis. Much of the time I felt discouraged and had to fight with a victim mentality.

Ultimately, I chose to view my life circumstances as *precisely the right set of conditions* necessary for me to cultivate more faith, more inner peace, more patience, and a better understanding of life.

When I truly learned how to stay in the present moment instead of worrying about what might never happen for me, the possibility for healing and transformation appeared. I started thinking: *It is going to happen for me. I can trust this process. There is a reason why motherhood has been delayed for me. It will make sense at some point.*

Profoundly positive outcomes happened for the women who followed my lead. The patients who entertained the idea that there was a spiritual reason for their infertility became practiced at focusing on positive possibilities. They persevered month after month, staying determined to reach motherhood. Many opened their minds to donor eggs or adoption, and found peace with that decision at last. Over time, several hundred more women became mothers as they embraced the possibility that a spiritual journey was leading them to baby.

The goal of this book is to help as many women as possible reach that same fertile place of spiritual understanding and personal empowerment. Though it may not seem evident at first, there is always a magnificent spiritual unfolding that occurs while we transform under life's challenges, including the challenges that infertility sticks to us.

Deeper self-love and greater personal happiness tends to come to the women who have the ability to look beyond their poor lab values and grim prognoses. If we change the way we view infertility; to see it as an opportunity to know and love ourselves, then we will see clearly what we need to be happy *before* we become parents.

Stick It to Me, Baby! presents the various spiritual concepts I have used successfully for years to help women reframe and transform the disappointments that come with infertility – disappointments that may include miscarried babies, as well as the heartbreak of lost children.

After implementing these concepts, infertile women gain sufficient self-mastery to change their perceptions of their situations, and subsequently, their outcomes. In essence, they allow infertility to change their lives, forever for the better.

We never have to feel "stuck" with the challenges that life or infertility presents. Rather, we can choose to embrace the path of infertility as a profound opportunity to awaken to the best of who we were always meant to be.

Let's begin to do that now...

Chapter 1

The Uterus Is Our Second Heart

The first concept I recall learning in my post-graduate level Chinese gynecology class was "the uterus is the second heart." This powerful notion now forms the cornerstone for my entire practice, and affects the way I view nearly all women's issues, particularly infertility.

According to Chinese gynecology, the uterus is situated energetically somewhere between the heart and the kidney organ systems, and reflects our attitudes about the emotions associated with each. The heart system processes joy and love, while the kidneys manage our fears. The degree to which a woman's uterus is fecund or pathological reveals the extent to which she has dealt with her feelings of love and fear.

Where there is a very deeply rooted fear, we absolutely will find a lack of joy; and when we truly love our lives as they are, the fear of being denied a joyful experience (such as motherhood) cannot exert power over us. But for many of us, the process of reconciling the old wounds and fears that have been stored for years is far from easy.

I've learned that Westerners in particular haven't been taught how to effectively move through pain, change, loss, or disappointment. Nor have we been told to expect transitions as part of a healthy and full life. We are only recently coming into the awareness of a mind-body connection that suggests our emotions directly impact our health.

For example, you may recall being told: "If you need to cry, go in the other room." Or: "You need to be strong right now." These messages may lead us to think other people know a better way of dealing with heartache, or that there is shame associated with expressing our feelings.

When the inevitable aspects of life occur (loss, disappointment, change), we often "store" the pain somewhere in our bodies. We feel confused about our emotions because we've been conditioned to believe it is best to keep our emotional vulnerability to ourselves.

With respect to infertility, ALL women have the same energetic connection between their head, their heart, and their womb. An emotion starts as a thought in our heads, then it's experienced as a feeling in our bodies. If the emotion is left unacknowledged it may take up space inside our wombs. Neglected emotional pain that is simply "stuffed down" will persist for years and can eventually manifest as uterine polyps, endometriosis, autoimmune conditions and fibroids – all of which hinder our fertility.

The uterus, as the "second heart," is meant to store joy and love like our heart center. But it's unable to do this in the case of infertility, where insecurity, fear, grief and unfulfilled desires compound and block our joy.

The scientific etiology of a uterine fibroid tumor begins with one little "seed" arising from hormone imbalance. Endometriosis similarly starts as one small adhesion, about the size of a freckle, that lands somewhere outside the uterus and spreads over time. Both of these conditions create structural barriers to fertility, and both arise from the mental seeding of a charged emotion mixed into an environment of imbalanced hormones.

Simply put, unresolved emotions must be transformed, released or reframed; they will not resolve on their own. Chronically ignored feelings become stored in your womb and potentially prevent you from becoming a mother.

It is possible to resolve our deeply rooted, unprocessed emotions. You can learn how to conquer fear and gain powerful wisdom from looking differently at your infertility. Set the intention right now to find more peace and joy in your life, thus allowing your uterus to become a more welcoming place for a baby.

My Fascination with Menstruation

One thing I've learned about women in the years that I've so intimately worked with them, is that enormous healing can come from sharing a powerful story at the right time. Well-told stories inspire, provide much needed perspective, and get us thinking. My personal story is woven through these chapters to help women feel safe applying these concepts to their own lives, and giving them permission to be vulnerable.

When I was about eleven-years-old I developed an interesting obsession with the onset of my first menstrual period. My behavior possibly suggested a future that would include educating women about *their* periods. But at the time, my eagerness to buy maxi-pads, etc., was a little odd. I was petite and felt underdeveloped compared to my friends, and longed for a more mature appearance. I believed that having a menstrual cycle would change my life drastically for the better.

Those days, my mother was an overworked, single parent with few resources. She was constantly stressed about money and experienced continual anxiety about raising two kids in poverty. She was a proud woman who kept our circumstances a closely guarded secret. She taught us to rely on "God" to meet all of our needs. She relied on faith in miracles to put food on the table. I watched her worry constantly and it affected me.

I recall feeling scared as she attempted to manage so much nervous energy. Not surprisingly, I began worrying and stressing all of the time. By age thirteen, my heart was often filled with fear and anxiety.

I must have believed that "becoming a woman" would be such a significant change that it would give me more control over my chaotic environment. To be more of an adult would mean I could help my mother in more ways. So I prayed endlessly: "Please, God, don't forget about me. Please remember to turn on my uterus!"

On September 13, 1984, I had my first period. I called out to my mom, "I'm bleeding! It's a miracle!"

I remember distinctly feeling like my prayers had finally been answered; soon I would be a happy woman running on the beach, just like the lady on the old boxes of Stayfree maxi-pads!

Instead, my cycle had me cramping, curling up in a ball, applying heat packs, taking Midol, and missing school. I remember once having cramps so intense I actually vomited. I thought, "God, why are you making this dream such a nightmare?"

That is how and when my relationship with my uterus became antagonistic. I resented my womb for causing me so much pain. I didn't yet realize I was the creator of that pain in the first place, overwhelmed with stressful thoughts that wreaked havoc on my hormone levels.

My first spiritual lessons – "Don't force things, they happen in their own time" and "Don't wish for something too much" – came from my first period. Who would know that these early events and feelings surrounding my menstruation were intended to lead me down a healer's path? At the time, I could only focus on the deep sense of disappointment and how menstruation was so different than what I had imagined.

Ironically, my mother opted to have her second heart removed around the time I started having my period. At thirty-five-years-old she had a complete hysterectomy and entered early, medically induced menopause. She was given a diagnosis of endometriosis, which meant that I was genetically predisposed to have it myself. I'm sure that watching her live with constant stress predisposed me to develop the disease just as much as genetics.

In college, I had my first laparoscopy (an invasive abdominal surgery that allows doctors to view and remove endometrial adhesions and cysts).

Many years later, after my diagnosis of premature ovarian failure, I was still managing such terrible menstrual pain that I decided to repeat the surgery. My doctor removed over 200 adhesions — revealing how this hormonal and emotional imbalance, when left untreated, progresses over time.

Those 200 adhesions represented the number of times that I didn't make the best choice for myself. Often I'd said "yes" when I should have said "no." Those adhesions represented the number of times my previously low self-esteem had led me into compromising situations in which I was not respected. As a teen I began drinking. In college I engaged in unhealthy relationships and, in two instances, I found myself the victim of a date rape and sexual assault. I told no one and stuffed the shame somewhere deep inside.

My repeated surgeries and years of menstrual pain confirmed that I was hurting, but I had grown up with no frame of reference for *healing*.

It wasn't until I had my own women's acupuncture clinic and had successfully guided enough women through infertility that I realized that I, too, needed to work through emotional wreckage collected over a lifetime of heart-breaking or stressful experiences.

With proper guidance and a commitment to self-evaluation, I learned it's entirely possible to heal our broken hearts and reconcile our emotions enough to optimize our wombs for baby. I learned the most from my work with a trusted friend and office colleague, licensed acupuncturist and healer, Anna Werderitsch. Treatment with her is what ultimately led to the recovery of my second heart.

We used acupuncture to "balance" my energy. But much more important in my healing were the countless spiritually based conversations we shared about the interplay between women's feelings and their physical issues. The concepts introduced in this book were born from my conversations with her.

During each session together, we peeled away a bit more of the emotional disharmony I had stored in my womb. We agreed that working with so many patients helped me gain greater self-esteem and confidence. This, in turn, contributed to a successful practice, giving me a sense of security that my mother never experienced. These new feelings stabilized me and helped halt the further growth of negative thought patterns and, ultimately, endometriosis.

Anna and I used the wisdom gained from my personal experience to help other women heal their infertility. We saw firsthand that it *is* possible to make peace with our second heart. After helping thousands of women, we were able to define the emotional and spiritual parameters that help optimize a uterus to do what it is naturally designed to do.

Chapter 2

Aim to Be a "Well Woman"

Typically, patients arrive at my office (appropriately named Well Women Acupuncture) because friends and progressive doctors who know of our unique approach make a referral. Usually the women arrive with flawless makeup, wearing beautiful clothes. They look poised and confident. Within minutes, however, they reveal that infertility has them beaten down, exhausted, and depressed. They are at our office because they have nothing to lose."

I recognize where they are on their journey because I've faced many of the same obstacles and feelings on my own journey to motherhood. In fact, I often thought that if any of the patients knew what I was coping with in regards to my own fertility status, they would be stunned! They would know I truly understood their plight.

Living with endometriosis meant that my menstrual fluid was often black, full of clots, and paired with intense cramps that had me nearly fainting or running to the toilet to throw up from the pain. I had become a regular guest at my gynecologist's office, repeatedly showing up for his help to remove the black blood clots that were too big to pass through my tightly clenched cervix. With this type of unhealthy menstrual period and my diagnosis of early menopause; which included night sweats, headaches and "prematurely aging eggs," it would have been all too easy for me to believe that I, too, was beyond help.

I stoically worked with my patients, being their cheerleader, keeping my personal information to myself while continuing to work steadfastly with Anna. She held me accountable for my reactions every time I had blood work done or had an ultrasound that might suggest even more "bad news." She was there for me when I had surgery for endometriosis, and when I found out that my fallopian tube was blocked. When things were not going well, Anna would let me cry for a spell, and briefly allowed me to indulge a victim-based mentality. Then she would say, "Okay, now do you *really* believe that you aren't going to have kids? Do you *really* believe that you aren't going to be a mother, when you're mothering all of these women in your practice?"

This female friendship and bonding resulted in both of us learning how women will support each other in times of stress. We courageously declared that we would run the practice in a way that consistently utilized a unique phenomenon known as "oxytocin bonding" which happens when women connect with each other. We believed this unique emphasis in our practice would set Well Women Acupuncture apart from other acupuncture clinics. We were right.

To help myself, as well as my patients, I read every book I could find about ovarian health, while Anna taught me how to return to a more natural, "traditional" way of eating. She introduced me to important nutritional ideas, such as the ways in which consuming more good fat and minerals calms the nerves, while eating enzymes from raw food increases energy levels. Consuming "raw" foods contradicted what we were taught in Chinese dietary therapy, and at first was hard for me to accept.

Together we created a comprehensive, somewhat experimental plan of action intended to address my mental, emotional, spiritual, and physical imbalances. We agreed to take an approach somewhat different from more traditional Chinese medicine, believing the changes would support me better in our more stressful, modern times. At the same time, we encouraged our patients to try the same approach – we asked them to implement the same changes I was making, and the results were overwhelmingly positive.

As I maintained the good fats and mineral-rich diet and applied the psycho-spiritual healing tools generated from our conversations, my own cycles started to improve. First they increased in length from 21 days to 24 or 25 days. Finally, I reached a 28-day cycle! With herbs and new food choices, the black blood went away and healthy cervical fluid began to flow once again. Finally, my cramping and menstrual pain disappeared.

What I gained during this healing process was priceless. Doing this transformational work inside the walls of my own office was wildly symbolic, suggesting that all of us really do have everything we need *inside ourselves* to promote miraculous healing. We can make changes within and become healthy, fertile "Well Women."

After working with thousands of women over the past fifteen years, I have come to define a Well Woman as someone who knows her strengths and weaknesses, and views both as acceptable parts of herself. A Well Woman is excited to embrace new concepts, foods, or techniques that will improve her entire life and all her relationships, not just to help her get pregnant. When a Well Woman has a dream or a goal, she will put one foot in front of the other and head straight toward the fulfillment of that dream. A Well Woman will have faith in herself, a connection to a source of strength, and a "master plan" to get where she wants to be.

When a woman is reminded that she has a choice over her reactions and authority over her emotions, she begins to feel empowered and becomes surprisingly more fertile.

Feeling more in control of her body can alter a woman's thought processes profoundly. She tends to become pregnant more easily and maintain a full-term pregnancy at last. Or she comes to the conclusion that using donated gametes, surrogacy, or adoption will offer her the immense joy and responsibility of motherhood that her spirit craves.

When an infertile woman begins to view herself as Well Woman, she notices a sense of well-being that extends into other areas of life, even beyond her ability to have a baby. I've watched many Well Women learn to allow their entire lives to be changed for the better as they give themselves permission to be healthy, fertile, and happier in general.

Chapter 3

Know You Are Enough

People ask me all the time how I came to be an acupuncturist. I explain that at age twenty-five, I was a college graduate with a prestigious job in DNA research, whose stressful life had created various health issues. Debilitating fatigue, various body pains, sinus problems, and digestive complaints led me to the office of Dr. David Wells, a "holistic practitioner" in Encino, California.

I was looking for a nutritionist to help guide me through food allergies and asthma. When I arrived at Dr. Wells' office I noticed his unfamiliar credentials, "L.Ac." However, his last name — Wells — was how I desperately wanted to feel, so I took a deep breath and walked inside.

A very empathetic Dr. Wells listened to me for thirty minutes during that first intake. He asked a few thought-provoking questions before examining my tongue and checking my pulse. Then he asked how I felt about needles. That's when I realized I was sitting in an acupuncturist's office!

My Western doctors had diagnosed me with fibromyalgia, food allergies, chronic sinusitis, asthma, anxiety, and a mitral valve prolapse.

By the time I met Dr. Wells, I had been prescribed beta-blockers, inhalers, steroids, antibiotics, anti-inflammatories, anti-anxiety medications, and muscle relaxants. The medical community had basically thrown their hands up in the air. Some of them told me it was all in my head.

I always thought acupuncture was a little creepy, but I felt an immediate comfort and safety in Dr. Wells' presence. If acupuncture offered even a little relief from some of these conditions, I was ready to give it a try.

To my surprise, there was no pain from the needles, and it was anything but creepy! In fact, I was surprised at how easily I dozed off and had a nice rest. After my treatment that first day, Dr. Wells said something that none of the other doctors had told me before. "You are going to be better soon."

I believed him. Those appointments became the highlight of my week. In each session I got useful information about what I should eat. I felt calm, and I had more energy. Dr. Wells always offered a pearl of wisdom that somehow improved my life; I was intrigued. Rather than taking pills, I was participating in true healing.

Within six weeks of walking into Dr. Wells' office, my entire life had changed. At my first appointment, I weighed only 83 pounds and had nearly ten different prescriptions. During those six weeks of acupuncture treatment I gained 20 healthy pounds, returning to a normal weight for my height. I was given one bottle of Chinese herbs, which resolved my asthma and allowed me to stop using all the inhalers and decongestants. Just a few short weeks before meeting Dr. Wells, I had contemplated asking my doctor to order a wheelchair for me because fibromyalgia caused such severe pain in my legs. Acupuncture had completely restored the quality of my life.

In subsequent treatment sessions, Dr. Wells casually inquired about the unrewarding work I was doing in DNA research at the time. We discussed how it required more than forty hours of my week and starved my spirit. Occasionally he would ask about my relationships. His simple questions were intended to get me thinking about the choices I was making and how I was approaching my life. It was fascinating to me that this form of medicine employed an empathetic approach, using communication and relatedness! As a result, I responded very well.

The most defining moment of my life up to that point came during an acupuncture session. Dr. Wells asked me with genuine interest, and quite out of nowhere, "Why do you think *you are not enough?*"

For a few moments, I felt totally exposed. I had no idea I was outwardly exhibiting such feelings of inadequacy. He put into words exactly what I had been feeling for years. Not enough. But why, why was I feeling so "not enough"?

With loving wisdom and sage-like detachment, he left the room then, allowing me the space to ponder his question and enjoy my acupuncture-induced endorphin high. I laid there for the thirty-minute session trusting that the answer to his very straightforward question was somewhere within me. I waited for it to be revealed.

I knew I was over-giving in several areas of my life. I knew I wasn't getting what I needed and deserved in relationships, and I didn't feel like asking for more would make much difference. But why was I staying at a job that bored me to tears? What was keeping me in so many unfulfilling situations?

Thanks to Dr. Wells, I came to the important realization that I could figure out what I needed and make different choices. I could simply be myself and allow that to be *more than enough.*

I grew up believing I was supposed to struggle, and that life was hard — because that's what I observed with my mother. I had a subconscious programming of *lack* that had been running my life, I'd never realized it until Dr. Wells called me out on this thinking pattern. So many doctors simply wrote prescriptions, indirectly telling me: "Take this medication. The answer is outside yourself." The acupuncturist was the one who challenged me to think differently, saying: *There's something you need to think about and once you do, you will correct yourself.*

I use this logic with my fertility patients, especially the ones who believe their eggs are not good enough, or those who worry that they are not young enough, or that they have not started acupuncture treatment soon enough. I advise them to begin mothering themselves, and recommend they tell the child within, *Little One, you **are** enough. You will be a good enough mom. You are healthy enough. And you can take good enough care of yourself to be given a child to love.*

Allowing ourselves to be *good enough* is a vital step to take on this path to baby. Acknowledgement that life is *good enough* brings internal peace and quiets the mental chatter about what isn't working. If we focus on not being fertile enough, having enough eggs or being young enough to become a mother, we will create more infertility, and age even more quickly.

Once I saw myself as "enough," I could trust that I deserved good things. Soon I quit my unfulfilling job in DNA research and began a four-year Master's Degree program in acupuncture and Chinese medicine. While in school, I realized as a practitioner I wouldn't be expected to be perfect, nor solve everyone's problems. Making my *best effort* to help would be enough.

In training to be an acupuncturist, I pursued work I enjoyed. At last, I felt a sense of freedom, purpose and self-fulfillment, rather than resentment from working long hours doing something I found mundane and tedious.

Now in practice, I have seen repeatedly that this same logic applies to healing infertility. Accepting our lives (or realizing we actually LOVE the lives we've created) is sometimes what helps women get to baby, whereas before they've struggled endlessly.

In this context, the words "good enough" are synonymous with acceptance. Acceptance is vital to anyone on a spiritual path, but it is especially important if our current path has led us to infertility. As human beings, we're challenged each day to accept that sometimes the most important things in our lives, the things we desire the most, are going to elude us or show up in ways different than we planned. Infertility proves this to us, over and over. It's up to us, however, to accept the challenge and look for the good along the way, no matter how small it may seem.

Grasping the concept of acceptance, and of being enough, creates freedom for women trying to get pregnant. This has allowed several women I work with to ditch their perfectionistic tendencies and accept that "a baby" may manifest in a different form than they had ever dreamed. Perhaps it will require years of doctor-assisted intervention. Maybe he or she will arrive as an adopted child, or as a baby via donor eggs. A baby can even manifest itself in the form of doing something creative, like conceiving an idea and birthing it into a book!

'Enough' is as good as a Feast, is a Chinese quote I picked up inside a fortune cookie along my journey. I now pass this wisdom on to my patients to remind them if they can see themselves as enough, then they can choose to view their life in terms of the ways they already feel satisfaction and abundance.

Letting One Embryo Be Enough

At age thirty-four, Jasmine found our office through her Mind-Body fertility group. She was what some would call "a tough nut to crack." She had a sharpness to her that covered a softer, more vulnerable interior. As a child, she was a victim of an abusive alcoholic mother. Consequently, abusive men had been part of her relationship history. Though she was now a happily married adult, she maintained financial responsibility for her aging, ill, alcoholic mother.

Jasmine insisted that her experiences had made her strong. She explained that she had accepted her life as one with more struggles than most. However, she had transformed the grief and made peace with it all. Jasmine continued to keep faith in herself always. She reaffirmed often that despite her history, she *was* enough and plenty deserving of a good life now.

Outwardly strong, healthy, and beautiful, it surprised everyone when Jasmine managed to produce relatively few eggs, and had only one embryo dividing well enough to be transferred back during IVF. In fact, her doctor wanted to call off that particular cycle to try again a few months later.

Relaxing during acupuncture, she opted to not feel sorry for herself, or explain how hard her life had been, and how unfair it was to be her. Instead, she named her one embryo "the sole survivor," and explained optimistically that given her life's experiences, she had no reason to expect *this* part of it to be easy. I watched as she courageously moved from anger and disappointment, to complete acceptance in that instant. Feeling safe in the treatment room, she got the chance to declare to me how much she accepted her life. Doing this freed her from attaching too much to the outcome of the cycle, and allowed her to trust her life to unfold as it always had. Yes, her life was a little tougher than those of some of her friends, but it was fulfilling for her.

She went on to conceive with that one embryo, allowing it to be enough—a survivor like herself. She had an uneventful but healthy pregnancy, resulting in the birth of her son.

Chapter 4
Maintain a Balanced Life

Healing infertility requires balance. On one side of an imagined scale, you have the reality of your situation (statistics, age, male factor, low odds, etc.). On the other side of this scale, you have faith in yourself – the belief that you will beat the odds and get through this challenging time of your life. As the scale often seems so unbalanced, you may constantly ask, "How many times can I generate enthusiasm and believe my healthy baby is coming, when nothing seems to work and I feel like a failure?"

When I watch my patients go through fertility treatments, I imagine them as gymnasts walking on a tightrope. In both instances, the person focuses, taking one step at a time, while staying determined to reach the other side. The likelihood of failure (falling) is there, but too much energy directed to those thoughts will work against her. It does no good to think of previous attempts, what might happen this time, or how easily it appears to be happening for other people. This focus and perseverance is what creates Olympians from gymnasts, and makes fantastic mothers out of those who get to the other side of their infertility.

The philosophy of Chinese medicine is that balance is imperative to healing. Acupuncturists are trained to use our heightened sensitivity to detect subtle imbalances in electromagnetic fields. We manipulate needles and prescribe herbs to balance the "yin and yang" energies in our patients. We propose dietary changes to balance the body's acid and alkaline state, and we suggest probiotics to ensure proper balance between good bacteria and yeast overgrowth in the gut. We may even recommend the practice of *Feng Shui* to balance the energy distribution in your home.

For four years, acupuncture students learn the healing properties of foods, herbs, and an extensive map of acupuncture points, all of which, when used properly, guide the human body back to this place called "balance."

We learned that humans possess five emotions (fear, joy, anger, worry, and sadness), which also must be balanced for overall health. Our curriculum required us to participate in "self-cultivation" classes like *T'ai Chi, Qi Gong,* and meditation, so that we could experience first-hand what balance feels like.

Ultimately, we were taught a very specific skill set designed to place us in the esteemed position of educating others about the importance of a cooperative balance between mind, body, and spirit. Maintaining healthy balance while trying to create a healthy pregnancy against the odds looks something like this:

- *Mentally* — your mind reflects a state of peace; you can release undue anxiety or fear. You do not overreact to pregnant friends posting on Facebook; nor do you isolate, avoiding pregnant friends because you feel too depressed or jealous.
- *Physically* — your body feels light and healthy, you actually enjoy the foods that benefit you, and have minimal cravings for foods that cause further imbalance; you are free of physical pain and have sufficient energy to enjoy a moderate amount of exercise.
- *Spiritually* — you have the awareness of being on a journey of life experiences, which will include both wonderful and painful events. You have the understanding that, if a baby is not coming to you despite your efforts, there must be a reason why, and you are willing to look beyond the obvious.

Interestingly, when we are out of balance we will tend to crave the things that keep us that way! If we have glycemic imbalance, we crave sugar.

If we need rest, we crave caffeine. Likewise, if we have hormone imbalance, we may crave the dramas that give us a release of neurohormones. Feeling angry about friends or relatives who are pregnant before us can seem like a great way to gloss over deeper feelings of sadness and fear. But staying angry only keeps a person more out of balance.

I began to examine my own pattern of imbalance after I got my infertility diagnosis. My combination of endometriosis and elevated FSH meant I had an estrogen dominance pattern despite having almost no estrogen circulating in my bloodstream, which revealed how out of balance I had become.

My training had served me well enough to know that an imbalance of that sort came from a combination of perceived stress, overworking, excessive emotions, and a poor diet. It was time for me to make a conscious decision to allow the satisfaction of helping other women be the inspiration and motivation for me to restore balance and heal on a deeper level, myself.

Overworking may have negatively affected my hormone balance and contributed to my infertility, given to the physical strain of the long hours, but immersing myself thoroughly in helping other women is what I believe offered me a way "through" infertility. Helping other women make their way to motherhood actually restored my faith that someday I, too, would overcome a poor prognosis and carry a healthy child.

To correct my diet, I began asking myself all day long: *is this food going to make my hormones balanced or imbalanced*? Just like recovery from alcohol or any other substance, the healing process included an hourly check in with myself to make sure I was acting in my own best interest. After months of applying consistent effort to achieve hormonal and emotional balance, I could see that I was clearly on the path to reproductive health.

If you are wondering whether you need to cultivate greater balance in your life, ask yourself: Do I feel happy with my life most of the time? Do I feel physically vibrant in general, and able to participate in physical activities I enjoy? Do I take my body outside to absorb rays of sunshine and let it breathe fresh air? Do I make time to cook nourishing food for myself and eat alongside people I enjoy?

If you answered "no" to these questions, ask what might you need to do to access your best, most balanced self, before parenting a child?

Let this newfound wisdom about balance lead you to the middle path of "committed detachment" with respect to baby-making. This means you are absolutely committed to the process of getting or staying pregnant, or becoming a mother. But you are also able to detach enough from the outcome to enjoy your life as it is, or "in the meantime."

Evolving into healthier people, and possibly better parents, is all about recognizing the importance of staying balanced—-despite life's obstacles, frustration and setbacks.

Balancing Mind, Body, and Spirit

Kristina was twenty-six-years-old when she arrived at my office for her first appointment. Because of her young age, both of us expected results fairly quickly. Achieving balance is not always an easy task, despite how rewarding the payoff may be. This story may be the best example I have ever seen of what is possible when a woman allows her body to find its optimal balance.

When I first met Kristina, my main concern was her marriage. She complained constantly about her husband's limitations and family drama. There were disconnects in their communication and constant friction between them about his inability to provide what she needed emotionally. Every session included an emotional venting of this pent-up frustration. I learned that these patterns of constant disappointment existed with her parents as well, and of course, her in-laws.

Consequently, Kristina suffered from depression, Chronic Fatigue Syndrome, and latent Epstein-Barr virus. She made her situation worse by relying on simple sugars for quick spurts of energy. Her life had become a vacillating cycle of cleansing diets and sugar binges, which aggravated polycystic ovaries.

Every time she ate sugar, her insulin levels spiked drastically, causing disruptions in the communication between her pituitary gland and her sex hormones, specifically testosterone and luteinizing hormone (LH), which is responsible for triggering ovulation. This sugar imbalance led to irregular, anovulatory menstrual cycles, countless mood swings, and endless frustration.

After three years of talking about her problems and fully breaking down the patterns behind her habits, she grasped the importance of balance and its direct relevance to her fertility. At last she was ready to commit to living a more balanced life.

Shifting first in her course of treatment was the dynamic in her marriage. After dozens of failed cycles, this young husband learned from his wife's constant frustration the importance of emotional connection, and how to just stop and listen to her when she was upset. He actually became one of the most involved husbands I have ever met! He learned what made her tick and how to allow time for her tears. It was beautiful.

They decided to leave the Los Angeles area, preferring the cooler, more fertile environment of the Pacific Northwest where they had close family. Right away, she began making an effort to resolve the conflicts she held with her mother and mother-in-law.

The biggest challenge of her balancing mission: the elimination of sugar and commitment to a regular exercise regimen. Kristina announced that she felt balanced enough in the other areas of her life to make these things her next priority. Now she was ready to commit to doing whatever was necessary to balance her blood sugar and reproductive hormones, in order to have a successful ovulation and regular menstrual cycles.

Supporting her as a friend at this point, I remember when she called me with "strange" symptoms. Every day for four months she had been moderately exercising and reportedly sticking to a cleansing diet, but for some reason, she was experiencing "enormous" breasts and bloating, despite the fact that her scale revealed a weight loss of over ten pounds.

Having polycystic ovaries, she was used to missed periods, but this was by far the longest she had gone without bleeding. Confused, she took a home pregnancy test. After quickly deciding it was another negative, she phoned her reproductive endocrinologist, then me.

Knowing those tests can take a while to register sufficient pregnancy hormone levels, I suggested she repeat the test in another week before returning to her doctor for progesterone injections to onset her period. Given her symptoms, I was not too surprised the following week when she called to announce a positive test!

What was most surprising, however, was her sonogram two weeks later. Somehow, in the midst of exercising, cleansing, and truly focusing on balancing her life, this statuesque, six-foot two-inch, very long-waisted, amazing woman was already far along in her pregnancy. Her "sixth week" ultrasound (intended to confirm a beating heart and properly placed yolk sac) revealed a developing fetus, complete with arms, legs, spine, nose, and ear buds! Her baby was already five months old!

The point of this miraculous story is that when we live a balanced life, whatever it is that we are destined to experience can "miraculously" appear, because we are no longer obsessing about or losing energy to the final outcome. This woman was finally living a balanced life, tending to her wounds from the past, and nurturing herself in the present, rather than obsessing about the future. She continued to live a life of balance and gave birth to a full term baby girl four months later.

Chapter 5

Practice Letting Go

Pause from reading for a minute to hold your right hand in a clenched fist. Really squeeze it tightly! Look at it while it is closed. After a few seconds, open your fist to release the tension. Feel and observe your open palm. Can you notice the obvious differences between the two hands?

A hand that is clenched can allow nothing to get inside. An opened hand exposes several points on the Chinese energy pathway known as the "Heart Channel," reflecting emotional vulnerability and an ability to receive.

Think now about the rest of your body. Do you have tight hips, sciatica, shoulder tension, shallow breathing, TMJ pain, or constipation? All of these symptoms demonstrate a body's emotional inability to let go. These areas—the hands, hips, lungs, intestines, upper back/shoulders and jaw muscles—are where we tend to clench and brace ourselves for protection from what we think might harm us. Usually we do this without even knowing it!

Symbolically, sciatica and stiff hip joints represents a resistance to moving forward. Clenched fists reveal a reluctance to release and surrender to the unknown. Constipation literally describes a colon that is unable to let go of digested food. These physical manifestations result when a person holds tight to the idea of being in control of their life and everything that happens in it. Sound familiar? I see these conditions every day in practice, as "secondary issues" beyond infertility.

Clenching can easily become second nature as we unconsciously grip whatever feels safe and familiar, whether or not we are intended to have that which we are clinging to so tightly. The fear of things getting out of control dominates and makes a person hold on, until he or she realizes that to be in control is an unattainable illusion. Uncertainty creates so much anxiety, it may feel safer holding tight to what is familiar, even though it is painful.

People are usually unaware of their clenching. Many have a hard time accepting that there's a spiritual basis for the life issues that keep repeating. They will assert that there is nothing wrong with them or the way they move through life; it's everyone or everything else not going their way! "If only x or y would happen," they think, if only they were in control of things, then they could be happy.

I remember working with one woman who claimed to want children, yet her professional life (running her husband's business from home) was so busy and her schedule so tight that she took pride in telling me how she did not allow herself to sit on the toilet long enough Monday through Friday to pass a bowel movement! On the weekends, she explained, she gave herself time and permission to void. It amazed me that she thought she would have time for children in that tightly controlled schedule.

While that is an extreme example of a holding pattern, the rest of us are plenty guilty of resisting change and not trusting the process of our lives to unfold in a way that will make us happy. As evolving spiritual beings, we are here now as humans learning how to invite change into our lives, and grow from new experiences.

Instead of maintaining patterns rooted in fear, *infertility offers us an opportunity to fully experience and transcend that which we fear most*. Once we allow ourselves to go beyond our perceived comfort zone to directly face our worry, disappointment, and frustration, we can allow new things to come to us. The richer our lives then become.

I believe life is always playing out exactly as it was intended. If our life involves frequent loss, pain and transformation, it means it was set up that way to teach us something and/or help us grow spiritually.

For example, there is no history of infertility in my family. Both my parents came from families with three and four children. My aunts and female cousins all had at least two or more children. My Midwestern relatives were content to live productive, simple lives. They each followed the family tradition: —working, marrying young, and having kids.

Being my mother's daughter, I chose differently, clinging stubbornly to perfectionistic ideals and reacting to emotional triggers. My fertility, and my love life, suffered as a result.

When I was thirty-three-years-old and in the midst of healing my infertility challenges, I became deeply attached to the idea of a relationship that I thought was *the one* for me. "Max" was a doctor who worked in my office building. He was smart, funny, and fit what I believed represented the answer to my "woe is me" life history. The fact that we had completely opposite upbringings and professional perspectives did not seem so important at first. My musings of what our relationship *could be* was much better than what the relationship really was, and because I was young, I held tightly to this fantasy notion and overlooked many things.

While dating Max, I began experiencing a gripping pain in my side that wouldn't go away. Rather than being sympathetic, Max seemed irritated when I repeatedly mentioned having this pain. I stopped bringing it up with him and asked my gynecologist to order a hysterosalpingogram (HSG).

In this diagnostic procedure, dye is inserted into the uterus to see if it flows freely through the fallopian tubes without resistance. The test reveals blockages in the tubes. While I held myself tightly during the uncomfortable procedure, I watched as the technician tried numerous times to force dye through my right tube.

This blocked tube diagnosis came as no surprise given how tense I was feeling in my relationship. I was figuratively bracing myself, desperately trying to hold onto something that was not intended for me in the first place. I didn't want to admit the relationship wasn't right. I didn't want to start dating all over again. My clenched fallopian tube revealed how tightly I was hanging onto it on a subconscious level.

After the awkward procedure, I returned home to discover while I was at the radiology lab having my HSG, Max was breaking up with me via email! Such an impersonal form of breakup was coming from the same man who asked me to move in with him just two weeks earlier.

It took intensive therapy to recover from this heartbreak and to release my grip on the dream that I believed the relationship represented. As traumatic as it seemed at the time, this loss turned out to be one of the most important opportunities I've ever had.

So many epiphanies came to me after I was "forced" to let go of that relationship. I learned that people (including babies) come into our lives and sometimes leave before we are ready. The challenge is that *we have to allow them to leave.* Hanging onto someone because of what they represent in our world only creates more pain and prevents new loves from coming to us.

From my experience counseling others, I was able to understand that my subconscious grip on this relationship had created a physical blockage. Therefore, I sought to address the clenching pattern at its root and explored other areas in life where I "held on" to things that did not serve me well. The more I chose to let go and just let things play out as they are meant to, the more my physical issues resolved themselves.

I've found the releasing process to be equally important for my patients; if they're willing to let go of their dream of the ideal path to baby or the fantasy baby represented ("Life will be great once we're a family"), then they can find some freedom from their own self-imposed shackles.

Two things I recommend frequently to help patients gain the detachment necessary to live a life free of clenching are *open-ended journaling* and *focused breathing.*

Open-ended journaling involves getting a fresh journal or a stack of blank paper and a good pen. The tool works best when you allow yourself to write uncensored about ALL the issues coming up for you—all the anger, frustration, fears, hopes and hopelessness with respect to getting pregnant, and any other areas of stress for you. When your hand starts to hurt is when you are beginning to get to what is really bothering you. That is precisely when to keep going! It is crucial to write *through* the pain. Typing on a computer is not the same as writing by hand!

When your tears drip onto the page is when you should rejoice; that's when you have tapped into the stuff you are holding most tightly. Allowing yourself the freedom to write until you can no longer hold your pen is extremely cathartic and healing.

After writing until it is physically impossible, or until you have reached a state of peace, head straight to your paper shredder and LET IT GO, forever. Imagine that your worries are going in with the paper and literally being transformed into shreds of nothingness. The worries, fears, doubts and angry, frustrated thoughts no longer have their grip on you, as you have released them from your energy field. You can repeat this exercise as often as necessary.

The focused breathing exercise I recommend is equally important in learning how to release your grip on life.

When you feel yourself clenching, take in a long, deep breath of air, then release it slowly. On your next inhalation, imagine *pulling* in energy and positive thoughts that you feel will strengthen you. When exhaling, imagine being able to release "stuck" energy, thought forms, frustrations, patterns, and fears that do not serve you. Let them all go as you audibly sigh or exhale fully, pursing your lips to really "push" that toxic energy out of your system.

It can feel unfamiliar and terrifying to float in uncertainty, trusting the process of your life to unfold in the direction that is ultimately best for you. Yet we need to do that in order to get where we want to go in life. We cannot cling to outgrown relationships and thought patterns any more than we can stay in a child's size one shoe! We have to take risks, release fears, and allow all the new thoughts that come with spiritual growth. As we take deep breaths and throw our clenched fists wide open, we expose our vulnerability and see that we have the receptivity necessary to allow that which we want to come to us. How liberating!

Opening Up to Possibility

Ting was forty-three-years-old when she first arrived at the Well Women Acupuncture office. She had been married for three years, and spent two and a half of them trying to get pregnant. Twice she had conceived using ART methods, but miscarried both times, at eleven weeks and seven weeks, respectively.

Her intake with respect to fertility offered little reason to explain the miscarriages. Despite her advanced age, her FSH was low, at 7.7, and diagnostic procedures including ultrasound, hysterosalpingogram, hysteroscopy, and laparoscopy were all normal. Pathology reports from her DNCs also offered little information for her.

I found it interesting that Ting had symptoms of "holding patterns." She grinded her teeth, had intestinal cramping, and constipation. She also had cold hands and feet, indicating that her energy was stuck in the middle of her body, unable to flow freely out to her limbs. She was seeing a therapist, and practicing the exercise found most appealing to people seeking physical and mental flexibility—yoga.

Several times we spoke about journaling, affirmations, and finding activities for her to focus on, while simultaneously participating in her baby pursuit. Rather than revolving her entire life around getting pregnant again, she went back to work and took up some arts and crafts.

About six months into her acupuncture and having had a third false start/miscarriage, she found herself nearing her forty-fourth birthday. Ting began researching adoption and egg donation. My staff and I applauded her for finding the courage to consider this alternate route to motherhood. I found it interesting her path to getting married had also required her to maintain an unconventional relationship for several years, in which Ting and her husband had to live in different states while dating.

I opened her eyes to the fact that their very satisfying marriage had previously looked like a complete impossibility. However, the outcome of waiting so long to be together was surprisingly happy and fulfilling. While neither of them enjoyed being apart, the challenge strengthened them as a couple, making the delay worthwhile. I suggested a delay and alternate route to motherhood could be just as unexpectedly rewarding.

Four months later, Ting surprised everyone with her ability to open to possibility. She accepted her younger sister's offer to provide eggs! This route would require counseling for both women, as well as very open minds. When she miscarried again using the younger eggs, she sought the advice of a new doctor who tested for and confirmed the presence of fetal antibodies in her bloodstream, an autoimmune diagnosis, which also explained her previous losses.

From a spiritual perspective, the diagnosis of "autoimmune" reflects a battle waging within oneself, in which the body attacks its own cells. Ting's next IVF would require steroids and blood thinning medications from the world of science to prevent an attack on another fertilized embryo.

Ting's spirit required her to have continued faith in herself, and the confidence to believe it was safe to let go of disappointment, pain, and frustration. The combination worked, and she delivered a healthy full-term son using frozen eggs from her sister. At last, she stayed open and stopped rejecting possibility.

Had Ting remained clenched, she may not have created the opportunity to know that amazing little guy.

Letting Go Allows Spirit to Work Its Magic

The idea that holding tight to the reins of life will put us more in control and prevent us from experiencing pain was big for Alyssa. Every week she came to my office and dominated our conversations by asking endless questions that left me little time to offer my perspective or advice.

I knew having so many questions was her way of trying to find the perfect way to create a successful cycle. If only it were that simple.

I liked Alyssa tremendously. She had a quick wit and I sensed that, overall, she was quite fertile, but really needed to relax and *give in* to what was destined to come to her, versus trying to control every aspect of each cycle.

I'll never forget the day she came to her appointment armed with ten used ovulation predictor sticks taped to a poster board, so I could view her previous five days of morning and evening tests. She wanted me to confirm definitively that the stripes were progressively thicker and darker each day, indicating a likely successful ovulation.

Her husband was also coming to me for treatment of a sperm issue. I had much of his information documented in her chart, as well as many pages of her lab values from various blood tests and notes from her prior failed cycles. Being able to keep track of so many details had actually become somewhat of a chore for me in this particular case, because she included and analyzed every detail with such scrutiny.

The day things finally shifted in her treatment started much like any other day in my office. I was sitting at my front desk, reviewing my calendar and pulling patient charts for the day. I remember noting something a little bizarre. Her chart seemed to be trying to get my attention! As odd as it sounds, I noticed that, while all the other patient charts were tucked away neatly, hers was sticking out by over an inch, alerting my eye to catch her last name. "Phillips," I heard several times in my head. It seemed to call out to me, as if to be sure I was paying specific attention.

"Hello, Phillips chart. I will see you at 3:00!" I acknowledged, thinking how strange it was to already feel a sense of impending dread at being unable to answer countless questions, having no better explanation than her doctor to explain why she was having such trouble conceiving at age thirty-six.

Imagine my horror when she arrived that afternoon and her chart was missing.

I scoured my desk, but it was nowhere to be found. I panicked briefly, wondering how I would be able to answer her deluge of questions. I grabbed a clipboard and blank paper, and proceeded to do her intake, answering questions from my memory, figuring the chart would appear after she left.

For five weeks, the chart's whereabouts remained a mystery. I managed to provide answers and effective acupuncture. By the fifth week, however, she was in a new cycle and would therefore expect me to have a different plan of action to help her feel more in-control and less anxious.

While waiting for her to arrive for her appointment, I took a few minutes to sit in meditation to calm my own thoughts of feeling out-of-control. Never before had I misplaced a patient's chart! I was too embarrassed and too stubborn to mention it to her. For four weeks, I kept her mindful of staying only in the present moment so I would not need to access my notes from her previous cycles.

As part of my training to be an acupuncturist I had electively been initiated into a lineage of Reiki practitioners. Reiki is a Japanese form of energy healing that can reveal information with the use of intuited symbols, openness, and heightened sensitivity.

Using Reiki had served me well in the past, as it enables me to receive insight and guidance for other patients, so I asked Alyssa if she was open to doing "energy work" that day. She said she was so frustrated that she was open to anything. She had no idea I had not seen her medical chart in nearly six weeks.

The instant I put my hands above her head to ask permission from her higher self to enter her energy field, I "saw" a symbolic heart with a healthy, growing fetus inside. Immediately I breathed a sigh of relief, shared the image with her, and noticed it gave her peace.

"Well, there is a little one coming. I clearly see a symbol of a heart, which I interpret as the womb. The uterus is the second heart, so for me to see a baby inside a heart symbol implies there is a baby spirit close to you. Very close."

She did not question me about how I knew this, or when baby would arrive. Instead, she rested peacefully on the table, so I continued the session.

After seeing the baby inside the heart symbol, I felt we were guided down a staircase into a room completely filled with paper. Boxes containing reams of documents were everywhere. Stacked on top of each other, nearly as tall as myself, these boxes seemed to contain what a person might interpret as important information; records of something. I explained this vision to Alyssa aloud and she stayed silent. I continued channeling the information being revealed to me.

"There is a typewriter here. An old-school typewriter. It's holding a piece of paper that looks as if someone has been typing a letter." I paused, then read the words to her, "Alyssa, let it all go. Dad."

She shifted on the table. I took a breath. "Does this have any significance to you? There are a lot of boxes in here. Do you know this place? Does any of it make sense?"

Alyssa calmly responded, "Yes. All of it."

I was seeing the imagery so clearly, I decided to keep going instead of asking her to validate and provide the story details. This allowed me to stay completely in intuitive alignment with the information I was receiving without my intellect taking over.

The energy expressing itself through Alyssa was using me to convey an important message to her. I was instructed to tell her about five specific items (a wine stopper, letter opener, something monogrammed, a framed picture, and a paperweight.) She was to find those items and keep them, but release everything else in the room.

All the boxes and paper were to be shredded and released permanently. "By the 17th of January," the voice declared. That was only three short weeks away.

It was then implied her next ovulation would occur that day, and if she had succeeded at letting go of all the documents, she would conceive a boy with a name starting with the letter "J." This was, by far, the most detailed Reiki session I had ever conducted!

One additional image seemed relevant to her success: a large aquarium with blue marbles. The final piece of information was an image of a man with a thick mustache, named James. His energy felt very satisfied and quite amused by the whole experience. I assumed this was her Dad, and she confirmed. "Yes, my dad's name was James Phillips, he was always playing jokes and he had a mustache."

"What do all these boxes have to do with you?" I asked.

She explained that her dad died very young and she always believed there was a piece of information missing about his passing, suggesting his death was wrongful in some way. Her intention was to go through a storage room full of paperwork to solve a mystery. The monthly expense of the storage rental drove her husband crazy!

She was stunned by the amount of information I was able to give her, and overwhelmed at the thought of disposing of so much paper, which she had been saving for over fifteen years. I told her it must be time to let it go, and she would find the energy to pull off this enormous task.

I left the room and headed out to my front desk. Just then, my assistant turned to me and said, "Hey, haven't you been looking for the Phillips chart?"

"Yessss," I replied slowly.

"Well, here it is." She handed me the chart. I laughed out loud.

When Alyssa came out of her treatment room, I finally told her my secret.

"Your dad has quite the sense of humor. He hid this chart from me five weeks ago. I had no choice but to do Reiki with you today. He is obviously happy now, because he allowed the chart to be seen; it was misfiled and your husband's chart was next to it, also in the wrong place. Your dad really wanted to get this message to you!"

As the weeks passed, she and her husband made countless trips to their storage unit. Working together, they managed to find the five items she was told to keep, and they destroyed the rest!

On the 17th of January, she visited her fertility doctor – her IUI was to be on that day, just as we had been shown in the session! In the lobby of this doctor's office was a big aquarium, lined with blue marbles.

Two weeks later, she returned to my office with a positive pregnancy test! Nine months after that, she delivered a boy and named him Jonathon.

Chapter 6
Find Faith within Yourself

Infertility asks us repeatedly to strengthen our faith and search deep inside ourselves — to see if we can keep trying, keep trusting, keep believing. In its simplest definition, to have faith is *to whole-heartedly believe in that which we haven't seen materialize in our lives yet.*

When we're able to trust our dreams are *in the process of* coming to be, we reveal incredible faith. And when we have faith, we are able to trust we'll be given everything we need at the right time.

Having faith goes beyond being hopeful. Hoping something will happen is simply too passive. Most people need to actively put energy into creating what they want in life, and that's what faith looks like. Having the courage to leap into the unknown or to sit still during an uncomfortable time are two ways we actively demonstrate our faith.

How can you develop greater faith that you will someday mother a child? I suggest reviewing your past—to specifically look for other tough times and situations that built your character; or other times when you felt put to the test. Recall other situations besides infertility in which you felt a need to be strong or patient. That's when your faith was tested.

To bolster my own faith in my body's ability to have improved fertility, I relied on sticky notes with insightful or inspirational affirmations. These bright little missives were posted in my bathroom and kitchen to remind myself several times a day that, despite countless heartbreaking relationships and the list of fertility challenges, I would eventually have the experience of raising at least one healthy child.

I told myself constantly: "ALL roads are leading me to motherhood."

That one sentence rang true for me, and it helped me accept what seemed like detours and dead-end roads. Repeating that sentence frequently increased its power and my faith in myself.

About one year after my unrealistic relationship with Max ended, I reviewed the way my life was unfolding. I was thirty-four-years-old, a time when everyone I knew was either getting engaged, married, or having a baby.

However, I was still immersed in therapy and kept busy attending workshops about how to attract a healthy man by being a healthy, happy, empowered woman.

I was determined to face my deepest fears and emotional triggers. Frequently, the old, negative thought forms would pop into my mind: *I'll never have what I want. I'm too much like my mother, so I will always struggle. My friends achieve their dreams, but I can't.*

I committed to regularly pushing that stream of negativity aside and stayed focused on keeping the faith that, just as each friend and patient had done, I would also find a man who wanted to try to have children with me. I had to have faith that it was all happening; everything was getting worked out, though I couldn't see it demonstrating at the time. I somehow knew that I needed to maintain unwavering faith in the possibility that the *right conditions* were being set up that would allow my dream of motherhood and partnership to become my reality.

It was difficult to work with some of my patients during this time. They appeared to have what I thought I couldn't attain — a supportive marriage in which they worked together toward their important goal of having a baby. I recall getting emotional when certain caring patients inquired how I was doing, because I was so vulnerable at the time.

My personal situation gave me a huge opportunity to relate to my patients' pain and vulnerability. I could truly appreciate their disappointments, struggles, and lost dreams. Like them, I often had thoughts of, *Why not me? Why can't I get what I want? Life isn't fair.*

Time and again, I opted out of self-pity and held the patients to that as well, insisting that we find faith in a bigger picture, imagining that something meaningful would come from surviving this uncomfortable time.

I began suggesting that affirmations I used that could also help them keep the faith. I told the women to tell themselves: "The right child is coming to me, at exactly the right time."

While prescribing faith-based affirmations, I reflected on the many times in which I faced challenges and came out better in the end. I reminded myself of times when I gave up on a dream — only to see it later replaced by something far better than I would have imagined!

Take a moment to remember some of your toughest times. Then fast-forward in your mind to the outcomes of those situations. Recall vividly a few times when life was sticking it to you hard, and how you emerged a better, stronger person. Remember how everything worked out in the end?

You can consciously choose to keep the faith that family building is happening for you, even when it appears to be the contrary. Affirm that baby IS coming to you – perhaps in an unexpected way, through some unexpected miracle or unexpected change that you have yet to see – then keep the faith in that idea.

Having Faith Creates "Faith"

"Leap, and the net will appear!" was a message that a very pregnant Rochelle scribbled on a sticky note for another patient she had met in our waiting room. However, when I first met Rochelle several months prior, she was one of the most doubting, fearful patients I had ever encountered.

She had miscarried the summer before coming to the Well Women office. After many months of trying again naturally and being unsuccessful, she sought help from one of the leading fertility clinics in the country, California Fertility Partners. Her doctor, the legendary Dr. Joyce Vargyas (who has passed away since the time of this story), referred her to me, suggesting a few treatments to calm her frayed nerves.

At the first appointment, Rochelle explained that she had already seen another acupuncturist who had a good reputation for helping women with fertility. She told me that this female Asian doctor took one look at her tongue and said, "Oh no, with that tongue you will never get pregnant!" I cringed upon hearing this, imagining how terrible Rochelle might have felt receiving that feedback from a last resort, alternative medicine practitioner.

My job, if she trusted me enough to try acupuncture again, would involve finding ways to restore her faith. Her husband was present and he liked what I had to say. He agreed to support any ideas I suggested during her sessions.

Despite the negative prognosis from the other acupuncturist, I really did not see the same unlikeliness of her conceiving. Instead, I saw a woman who was letting a lot of fear get in the way of having what she wanted. I asked her to focus her attention on the fact that she had become pregnant easily and to remember that, unfortunately, miscarriages sometimes occur during the process of family building. Her doctors tried to reassure her based on the fact that her miscarriage was due to chromosomal abnormalities. They repeatedly told her that at thirty-five-years-old, miscarriage was unlikely to happen again.

I remember the lengthy negotiation involved to convince Rochelle to relax and try naturally for six months before trying IVF. I really believed that she was a woman who simply needed more faith in order to conceive again naturally and sustain pregnancy. It was very difficult for her to believe that full-term pregnancy was a possibility for her, after having lost one pregnancy. Regardless, she stepped up to the challenge and agreed to trust my expertise and try it my way for six months.

Near each ovulation, she tried hard to relax. She joked that she and her husband would have good sex (vs. baby-making sex) as many times as possible. Then each month she got her period, she would question me endlessly, "Are you sure, Danica? Are you sure taking a break from IVF is the best thing for me? Are you sure it's all about trusting? Are you sure I just need to keep the faith?"

I volunteered to keep the faith it would work, until she was able to hold that reality for herself. I let her know although I didn't have the definitive answers she was looking for, it seemed pretty clear the *worst* thing that could happen was she would be using the time before IVF to get herself in good shape with some acupuncture and herbs.

Three months into this test of faith she got a positive pregnancy test!

One slow week at a time, the pregnancy tested her faith over and over. Could she keep the faith? Would she make it past the ninth week, at which point she had previously miscarried? Then, would she make it through the first trimester, and all the way through the pregnancy... to eventually hold a healthy baby in her arms?

There were little scares along the way. I guess they could be called even more tests of faith. At her due date she delivered a healthy baby girl, and named her, quite appropriately, "Faith."

Cultivating faith in her heart led her to hold Faith, the child, in her arms. It was an awesome blessing that did not stop there. She conceived again spontaneously when Faith was only eight weeks old! Rochelle had created a new belief — "conceiving healthy babies can be easy" — and she put her faith into that belief during the second pregnancy.

However, old fears about miscarriage resurfaced to test this new belief system. She chose to remind herself about her body's ability to grow one healthy child already, and she looked to her daughter as the living proof that being a mother was definitely part of a master plan for her life.

Now, she's a mother of *three* children. Her experience demonstrating the power of faith allows her to share the message: "Leap, and the net will appear." The positive impact from her personal journey ripples outward to others. The woman in the lobby who received the sticky note message from Rochelle also became a mother, after putting her faith into a donor egg protocol.

Start writing your own inspirational sticky notes to help you keep the faith. These appropriately placed mantras can serve as helpful reminders along your journey that if you want to reach motherhood, *all* roads are leading you there.

Chapter 7

Want It for Others

Infertility really sticks it to us when friends flaunt their seemingly effortless pregnancies on Facebook, and when we have baby-focused events to attend. As our sights become set on having a healthy baby to love, we begin to notice every single woman pushing a stroller or sporting a swollen belly. How frustrating it is to be unsuccessful each month, while it appears so effortless for others!

There's considerable conflict inside a woman who believes she has done everything possible to get pregnant when it looks like it came so easily for someone else. These conflicted emotions can include feeling inadequate, broken, sad, jealous, guilty, hopeless, or unworthy.

Infertile women *are* happy for their friends. But the instinctual longing to push their own stroller and know their own babies is intense enough to cause physical and emotional pain the longer the experience is denied them. This pain is typically described as a visceral feeling in the chest or womb, typically noted as "a deep ache." The ache relates to the empty, unoccupied space in their hearts where these women feel their child is supposed to reside.

Even if this physical sensation lifts, many women still hold guilt about having negative, jealous thoughts. They fight back tears while they're getting ready for a baby event or when they have to select another woman's baby gift.

What makes matters worse is the barrage of unsolicited opinions, pity, or advice that women face at these events. Friends may say well-meaning things like: "You just need to let it go, then it will happen," or "When my husband and I took a vacation is when it happened for us." Though the intentions are good, these comments cause resentment.

"Infertile" women *have tried* in their own way to do such things! Hearing thoughtless suggestions creates animosity. Telling someone to "let it go," without explaining how, can be really upsetting!

In all fairness, baby-focused events can also be tough for the pregnant woman being honored. If a woman is conscious of her friend's feelings and countless failed attempts, she won't want to cause further pain. Being excluded from such events is equally hurtful. The whole situation can really strain or damage a friendship.

When I was a single woman who was dealing with infertility and having no luck getting married, I was invited to over a hundred such joyous occasions (various women's showers and weddings). I had numerous chances to explore what triggered me emotionally, and I heard similar stories from my patients. I was learning that there are ways to reframe the pain from these social situations.

Instead of feeling resentful, I decided to view these events as opportunities to experience a spiritual connection with other women. I also focused on the fact that these women had succeeded in directing their lives to good partners and healthy babies. I concluded that these women and their celebrations could teach me something I might be missing.

I finally got over my own emotions enough to realize that these events were about sharing good feelings and supporting one another through huge transitions, while welcoming precious babies into the world. Before consciously reframing my perspective, I struggled with unhealthy thoughts of jealousy, irritation, feelings of doubt and defeat, all the while comparing myself to others. That was an unhealthy way of coping.

I realized that if I made the choice to be happy for my friends and encouraged my patients to be happy for their friends, the healthy bonding between women would likely get us *all* to our desired goals, perhaps much faster—and with a much more loving disposition.

After all, the process of conceiving and birthing a child is a beautiful thing. Successful pregnancy truly IS a miracle. Instead of feeling jealous, we can try to feel inspired and encouraged for ourselves when we receive news that the miracle of conception has happened for someone else.

If we can change our perspective, we can allow our friends' announcements to motivate us to keep shifting and allowing more positive change. Baby bumps and showers confirm that healthy pregnancy has happened for other women, which means it can happen for the rest of us.

Try to entertain that possibility. Participate as fully as you can at the next celebration you attend for a child who is on his or her way! Find joy in providing him or her with some nice clothes or cute toys. Focus on the excitement of transitions and dreams being fulfilled... so it can someday happen for you!

From a spiritual perspective, we need to raise our vibration to match the same vibration of the things that we desire. We must allow ourselves to be aligned with our own desired fulfillment. When we are excited for someone else who's having a baby, it implies that we, too, will experience the joy of others being excited for us.

In fact, science would say that we raise our fertile potential by being happy for mothers-to-be, and by being excited that there is a little being coming into the world. Being happy raises serotonin levels in the brain, and tells the ovaries that "all is well," which makes us more fertile.

We always have the choice to receive other people's good news with joy, no matter what our circumstances are. Comparing ourselves to others can leave us feeling empty, judgmental, victimized or negative. It thwarts our ability to keep our hearts (and second hearts) open to what is coming to us. Now, why would we want to do that?

If you find yourself feeling hurt or angry about another person's good fortune, try going a little deeper into self-evaluation to find out why. Besides a baby, what else might you need to feel happier in your life? Think on that for a while; allow the most honest answer to come to you, and strive to create that for yourself.

Welcome, Baby Annika!

Greta and Aaron, a young Mormon couple, were constantly surrounded by pregnant friends and frequently invited to large family-centered celebrations. For four years they had been trying to get pregnant. Both Aaron and Greta experienced significant transformation as they walked the path of infertility. Though it nearly destroyed their marriage, they each became strengthened – emotionally, physically, and spiritually from the process.

Three years into their journey, they managed to save enough money to try one IVF protocol, which Greta regarded as their last resort. She didn't want to attempt IVF; thinking that, if science failed them, they would truly be hopeless. However, she felt better with the money reserved for IVF, "just in case."

At the same time, her older brother and his wife were also having trouble conceiving. Although they had not tried as long as Greta and Aaron, they were older, which could make the process more challenging.

I was speechless a few months later when Greta informed me that they had offered their baby savings to help her sister-in-law do IVF!

This by far is the best example I have ever seen of someone truly wanting it for others. What selfless generosity, and what faith they demonstrated! Their actions proved that they wholeheartedly believed that someday, somehow, they would find their way to their child!

As it turned out, Greta's sister-in-law conceived that same month and did not need an IVF cycle, after all. After offering her brother the funding for IVF, Greta learned that her irregular cycles had actually facilitated a "surprise" pregnancy, leaving the two women stunned and pregnant at the same time.

Of course, we will never know if Greta and Aaron's generosity helped her sister-in-law feel supported, and therefore more relaxed and receptive in that cycle. But something definitely shifted for Greta and Aaron when they demonstrated such faith, and placed their family members' happiness above their fears that their own pregnancy would never happen.

Greta chose the name "Annika" for her baby girl. She says that every day when she speaks her daughter's name, she acknowledges the friendship, support, and spiritual guidance she received while working with Anna and me at Well Women all of those years!

If this story inspires you enough to feel interested in actively helping another person fund their fertility journey, make note of the non-profit organization called Baby Quest Foundation. For more information about donating to this cause, or to apply for a grant for help with funding, visit www.babyquestfoundation.org.

Chapter 8
Trust the Process

Being able to trust that life will unfold how we want it to and result in the happy ending of a healthy baby can require the utmost faith and confidence. High-tech, "assisted" protocols often require women to place a lot much trust outside of themselves, usually from a place of desperation. However, being able to trust yourself, your body, and your inner voice as much as you trust your doctor, is a crucial aspect of resolving infertility.

Making the choice to view family building from a spiritual perspective involves being able to trust in a "master plan." Seeing the bigger picture can give you the ability to believe that the process is unfolding for you in perfect timing, and with the best outcome possible.

When we fully trust, we feel safe relying on "something bigger than ourselves" to completely take care of our needs. We can let go of our need to control how something should come about, what it needs to look like, and when we need it to happen. By trusting and surrendering, we are saying, "Okay, God/Universe/Divine Spirit, I thought now would be a good time to have a baby. But since it's not happening, I will again trust that *if and when* I am supposed to become a mother, it will happen as if it's the most natural thing in the world. I can trust that I'm with the right person to join me in this endeavor. I'll be guided to the right doctors, too, if that's what is necessary. I will trust, in order to keep my spirit lifted and my heart open. If there are changes that I need to make along the way, I trust that I will receive clear guidance."

Trusting reduces our doubts and creates a sense of safety. When we completely trust a situation, we stop questioning everything so much.

When we trust that we are cared for is when it's easiest to be our best, most relaxed selves; which is typically when life's biggest rewards come to us, anyway. In the years I've worked with infertile women, there has been a clear distinction between those who can trust the process of becoming a mother, and those who cannot. You can guess which type ends up pregnant more frequently...

Positive-minded women generally find it easier to trust because they review their lives in terms of how positively things have turned out in the past. With confidence, these women trust that more contentment is in store for them in the future. A woman with a negative perspective, however, will stay rooted in fear and resist trusting the process. She lets her negative past experiences and fears suggest that her future is destined for more pain, disappointment, and loss.

Is trusting easy? Well, not usually.

Trust is built over time, and it grows when we review our lives in search of all the times things happened just as they were intended. Looking objectively at your life will illuminate that it is probably important for you to trust again now, at this difficult time.

Sometimes we need tools to help us stay open and trusting while we're on a spiritual path to baby. I love reading inspirational books by authors such as Wayne Dyer and Michael Bernard Beckwith. Their insight helps me stay focused on spiritual truths, especially in the most challenging times. Their words restore my trust in a divine unfolding of life and remind me that we are always connected to an abundant source of spiritual energy that wants us to be happy. Reading a passage from any one of their inspirational books quickly reminds me that the universe is always providing what I need. If it's hard for you to trust this process, take a moment to ask yourself:

- Whom do I trust?
- How did I learn to trust?

- Was my trust in someone ever violated?
- Once lost, did I get trust back?
- Do I trust too soon, or hold such high standards that no one is trusted?
- Do I blindly trust my doctors?
- Why do I not trust the universe to give me/us a child?

If you've lost trust in yourself, your reproductive abilities, or your faith, ask yourself honestly *what would it take* (besides getting pregnant) to allow you to trust again?

Courage and confidence are the two components necessary to build trust. Can you find those within yourself by recalling how your life experiences have unfolded already?

Interviewing for an important job, auditioning for an acting role, taking a licensing exam, completing a marathon, moving to a different country, choosing a life partner, getting married –or perhaps going through a divorce, are all good examples of times when you had to rely on trusting yourself to get through intense moments on your own. No one else filled in for you at those times.

Let this truth remind you that you *can* trust your life to unfold as you intend, especially when you back it up with faith. Surviving challenging experiences shows us how capable we are! Trust that "infertility" is no different.

One thing is certain about the fertility journey. It presents plenty of tough decisions. Which clinic should we work with? Is it time to start medication? How aggressive should we be with protocols? Is there a necessary surgery to consider? Do we need to use donated gametes? Who is the right egg/sperm donor? When is it best to use a surrogate? When is it time to call it quits?

Every one of these important decisions has the potential to first challenge you; then reveal an opportunity to deepen your trust that every day, in every way, you are moving yourself in the right direction.

Marilyn and I Learned to Trust Together

On my first day of student internship, Marilyn came to see me as a patient. She was thirty-eight-years-old and stated that she wanted to have a second child. This was Marilyn's first acupuncture treatment. Obviously, she had no idea that it was my first day treating "real" patients. Neither one of us could have possibly known that our lives were about to change drastically following that appointment!

During her intake, I learned that she was lacking "qi" and "blood," two vital substances necessary for healthy conception and pregnancy, according to Chinese medicine. Usually, a nutrient deficient diet will cause this scenario. Marilyn had also become deficient in qi and blood from nursing her daughter. I advised her to reduce refined sugars and increase her intake of mineral-rich leafy greens, and suggested she have more meat protein.

After giving this dietary advice, the treatment began. Marilyn was a somewhat nervous woman in general, and this first treatment elicited a strong sensation for her, causing her to become anxious and hyperventilate. Not wanting to frighten her more by announcing it was my first day in the clinic, I quickly removed the needles, then calmly asked her to sit up and take deep breaths through her nose. We got through the experience together and, twenty minutes later, she left the clinic feeling better.

The next morning, I called her to follow up. I asked her to trust me as I suggested a different course of treatment, using fewer needles and avoiding the point that had created such unease and anxiety for her. She appreciated my concern and professionalism, and agreed to trust that the panic attack would not occur again. She returned the following week.

An acupuncturist will check a patient's pulse to assess the state of the body's qi and organ systems. The pulse thickens or thins, speeds up or slows down, and varies depending on a patient's pattern and circumstances. On the day of her second treatment, I felt my first "pregnant" pulse! I asked Marilyn if she could be pregnant already, despite the deficiencies noted during her initial appointment. She announced she couldn't be more than 9 days past ovulation and marveled at how I could possibly entertain such information from her pulse!

Her treatment on that day was otherwise uneventful. She didn't have another panic attack, and we agreed to speak the next day to see what a home pregnancy test revealed.

When I called her the next morning, she was elated. I had been entirely accurate with my pulse diagnosis. She was, indeed, already pregnant. The test picked it up, and it was not even time yet for her menstrual period to begin!

I worked with Marilyn every week of her pregnancy. At that time, I had no idea I would someday work primarily with pregnant women, and particularly those trying to conceive. I simply trusted that something big was happening for me because of this woman. Because of the connection between us, I wanted to learn as much as I could about what happens to a woman's body and fetus during each week of pregnancy.

I trusted that there was a reason she was my patient, and she trusted all the while that the needles were good for her and her unborn baby.

She delivered a healthy baby boy a few months before I started my own practice. The overall experience was good for her in so many ways. She said it kept back pain and anxiety down during pregnancy, while keeping her energy up. She constantly told her friends and family about me, and shared the enlightening experiences we had together.

As it turned out, Marilyn's enthusiasm about her treatments was contagious. Her unexpected good experience with acupuncture spread wildly to other enthusiastic friends, which soon generated nearly 60%

of my client base. At one point early on in my career, the majority of my patients could be traced back to this one woman as the source of the referrals!

We shared a mutual trust and belief that our paths were supposed to cross, affecting us each in different and unforeseen ways. Her son is now a young man. Over one-thousand children have come into the world as the direct result of the knowledge I've gained and the trust I have in my diagnostic abilities. I strengthened both of these abilities while accompanying Marilyn during that pregnancy. The process continues to unfold perfectly, revealing that the journey to baby can be made somewhat easier when women decide to trust themselves.

Chapter 9
Learn to Calm the Mind

In Chinese medicine, we say that worry "knots the qi." Round and round in our heads go the obsessive thoughts and worries we process all day long. These thoughts get us nowhere, and often yield nothing but a gut-wrenching feeling in the pit of our stomach.

Over-thinking is a symptom of a weakened "spleen system," according to Chinese theory. When the spleen energy is weak or deficient, we lose our ability to transform food into new qi and blood. With respect to fertility, obsessing about things we have no control over metaphorically knots our reproductive energy and lessens our ability to make the nutrients necessary to nourish our womb.

This concept is important for the women out there who spend way too much time analyzing their BBT charts and IVF calendars, or indulging every one of their worries about not being able to conceive. There is a destructive potential to this kind of excess thinking.

Women with weakened spleen energy appear tired, pale, usually with flabby muscle tone. They typically suffer from mild depression, rely on sugar for energy, and tend towards anxiety. Friends frequently have to calm or reassure these worriers. They often have digestive trouble that is further aggravated by stress and worry (i.e. nervous stomach, irritable bowel, colitis, weight gain, or lack of appetite, etc.).

What these worried women don't know is that their thoughts can be *redirected* — in a way that practically ensures improved fertility!

Consider that, if women who typically obsess and over-think chose instead to direct all those worried thoughts to beliefs of *certainty,* they could begin manifesting anything they want! Our thoughts are that powerful.

We think upwards of 50,000 thoughts per day. Many of these thoughts are concentrated on fear, doubt, or worry. However, we have the power to train our minds to focus instead on trust, faith, and confidence. Imagine if you began focusing 50,000 thoughts per day on the *fulfillment* of your desired outcome...

I was told before age thirty-two that I would not be a candidate for IVF unless I used donated eggs. At that time, I was busy working ten-twelve hour days, fervently treating an average of fifteen infertile women each day. Those hours were spent wiping tears, listening to stories of worry, tragedy, frustration, disappointment, and despair. I was helping in whatever way I could to restore their faith and help them trust in themselves, and their bodies. On top of my own 50,000 thoughts, I was exposed to an onslaught of worried thoughts from my patients.

That scenario was set up perfectly for me to adopt their worrying and doubt my own likeliness of becoming a mother. How easy it would have been for me to let fearful, anxious thoughts get the better of me. Instead, I posted mind-calming affirmations all over my home and office. I trained my brain to "obsessively" think thoughts of myself birthing a healthy baby and raising a healthy child someday! I reviewed my daily schedule to find other times where I could intentionally practice *reprogramming* my thoughts, as often as possible.

I like to wash my hands between each of my patient sessions. This habit presented me with at least fifteen opportunities to rinse my hands at the sink, and simultaneously rinse my thoughts of negativity and fear. In between each patient, I would rinse my hands, look in the mirror and tell myself clearly, "It is going to happen *easily* for me. I am the person in charge of my thoughts, and in this moment I am reminding myself that it is 100% likely that my body will create a genetically healthy baby when the time is right, with the right person."

What a difference those thoughts made! In fact, this is the mental practice that still allows me to continuously provide my patients with a positive outlook after each of their failed cycle attempts.

I have several tools that successfully help women overcome worry. One of the most powerful techniques is simply asking the question: *What if?*

That question brings each woman face-to-face with her worst-case scenario and helps her play it out to the end, at which point she realizes she'll be okay in any outcome.

For example, a patient may be getting stuck in the fear and worry loop of thinking, "What if this cycle doesn't work?" So we allow the conversation to unfold. "If the cycle doesn't work, I will probably start crying. I will be really sad. I will be scared that it may never work." And so on.

In hearing their answers out loud, they realize that even IF their worst worry does occur, they *will* be able to deal with it. They *can* pick themselves up and keep moving in a new direction. *If it doesn't work, then we may try to adopt. If it doesn't work, then we are done with our attempts and this madness can stop. If it doesn't work, then we will borrow money from our family and do it again. If it doesn't work, we may need to take a break to regroup.*

Eventually, they recognize that no matter what happens, life will not come to an end. Though disappointment is hard on us emotionally, we can handle another setback if it happens. This practice helps women stay in the present moment, dealing only with what is happening right now, not last cycle, or what might happen in future cycles.

Another calming tool I recommend asks that patients redirect their focus to something that IS working in their life, or I may ask, "What are some of the things you have learned about yourself while going through this process?"

Acknowledging the new personal strengths that infertility has offered (such as courage, patience, greater self-love, trust, or faith) brings a sense of peace, increased confidence, and a healthier perspective. This practice can guide women to not feel so victimized by their infertility.

Sometimes I ask women to list the various examples of wisdom they have gained from this process and the positive aspects of themselves they have discovered, that they would share with their child if he or she were here already. This exercise is powerful. It connects women to an unborn child "out there somewhere" and helps them refresh their memory about how wonderful and capable they are of nurturing a child.

Meditation is yet another tool infertile patients can use to become more aware of their tendency to worry. A consistent meditation or "mindfulness" practice truly calms worries, as people learn to observe and redirect their self-defeating, circular thoughts to a more direct, confident place.

Some women have a friend they frequently check in with who can hold them accountable for maintaining a relaxed state of mind. Taking a walk or having a calming acupuncture treatment can be a great way to trigger a wave of peace. Whatever methods consistently achieve the best results and allow us to ground our minds in "possibility thinking" is what I suggest.

Our minds and bodies work in tandem, so we must consciously nourish both throughout the process of improving our fertility. There's a classic Chinese recipe that acupuncturists use all the time to calm the minds of worried people with weakened spleen energy. It is sweetened with Chinese cherries to nourish the blood, and it contains herbs that help digestion and soothe anxiety. Anna and I created a modification of this classic and prescribe it frequently to women who have a hard time sleeping or calming themselves during this process. Women benefit almost immediately from taking a calming tonic, as well as from making changes to their diet.

Foods that "benefit the spleen" include warm squash, alternative grains such as quinoa and millet, and meat protein like beef, chicken, and turkey (soy protein does not have the same grounding affect and is actually not recommended for women trying to conceive due to its proven effect on estrogen levels). Avoiding cold foods, excessively sweet foods, and processed convenient foods (i.e. frozen meals) will lessen the assault on the spleen and help women think balanced thoughts, making them feel calmer in general.

Traditional Chinese medicine says "the spirit resides in the blood" and "the spleen makes blood." Therefore, if the woman's blood is deficient from weakened spleen energy due to excessive worrying, the spirit will wander, having no place to rest.

Therefore, a woman with adequate blood appears more grounded and can easily calm her nerves during stressful times, as she is accustomed to eating warm, balanced meals made of food that is not heavily processed with chemicals. Conversely, undernourished women who skip meals and rely on sugary, processed foods panic easily and worry often.

So many fertility patients suffer more than they need to and make their journey to motherhood more of a struggle by failing to nourish their bodies and minds with healthy food and calming thoughts. Evaluate your daily routine with respect to diet and behavior. Do you rely on chocolate, coffee, tea, or diet sodas for energy? Do you eat a boxed frozen meal for lunch and feel obsessed with worry that you won't be able to have a baby? If so, understand that you are working against yourself and making it harder to reach your goal. It's time to put that worried energy into making different choices!

Nourishing the Blood to Calm the Spirit

Jennifer was thirty-two-years-old when she had her first miscarriage. After one year of BBT charting and Clomid cycles, she decided to try acupuncture and Chinese medicine to see if they would help restore her body and increase her chances of carrying a healthy baby to full term.

I assessed her diet at the first appointment. Cold yogurt and fruit, diet soda, frozen lunches, and pasta comprised 90% of her food intake. She was tired, pale, and not ovulating successfully (despite Clomid use); her periods were scanty and ultrasound confirmed her uterine lining was consistently thin. As a second grade teacher, she often worried obsessively about lesson plans and maintaining control over her classroom.

Immediately, I explained the connection between cold, empty foods, worrying, and a thin uterine lining that cannot nourish a baby. I needled the points intended to restore and rebuild digestive energy. She was given herbs to "revive" her spleen, calm her mind, and start the process of building fresh blood.

She took the herbs for a month and reported having a menstrual period when expected that was heavier and lasted longer than normal. She had also weaned herself off the diet soda and started feeling calmer, less quick to worry. She noticed increased energy from the herbs and inclusion of mineral rich leafy green vegetables into her diet. She was sleeping better and waking up enthusiastic and refreshed. Jennifer's body was not only recovering from miscarriage; it was finally receiving the nourishment it so desperately needed for years.

After that first heavier period, she successfully ovulated. Jennifer waited calmly as weeks passed with no period. Her BBT chart suggested pregnancy, as her luteal temperature was rising steadily above 98 degrees. Blood tests confirmed she had conceived again, and this time pregnancy was successful! She received acupuncture throughout the entire pregnancy for back pain and to regulate her previously weakened digestion. Nine months later, Jennifer delivered a son.

One year and a half later, she returned to the office and admitted going back to her previous poor diet. Consequently, she had miscarried again while attempting baby number two. Complaining of mental restlessness and the inability to sleep, she mentioned again having a scant menstrual flow since she finished nursing (as breastfeeding typically makes women more blood deficient).

Once again, I prescribed herbs to restore the digestive energy to begin building blood. Her following cycle was heavier, her mood was improved, and ovulation occurred the following month as scheduled. The next month she again ovulated successfully and returned a few weeks later after confirming pregnancy!

She continued taking the herbs through the first trimester for extra nourishment, understanding that she had lost much of her vitality from a year of nursing, chasing her older boy, and working. This second uneventful pregnancy also ended with a healthy baby, another boy! Jennifer now understands that her life demands require her to stay nourished in order to feel calm and function optimally.

Chapter 10

Cultivate Patience

Quan Yin, a female Buddha, is always depicted sitting or standing inside a lotus flower cultivating Infinite Patience. Perfectly poised in serenity, her image serves as a reminder to humans of the inner fortitude of patience we all possess, yet so often forget.

Instead, our impatience and inability to see the natural unfolding of our lives makes us hyper-focused on our calendars and schedules. Our instant gratification society has created a panicky scenario for many infertile women that gets triggered each time they start their menstrual period. We fret over how quickly time is passing without pregnancy. Then we impatiently complain that time is moving too slowly during the twelve-fourteen days of the luteal phase, while waiting for a positive pregnancy test.

Impatience has us irrationally believing that we can force our bodies to conform to our dreams and deadlines. As a result, women turn to ART protocols, perhaps too quickly, then do one IVF cycle after another without resting in between. Often, the ovaries react to our self-imposed pressure by becoming "poor responders" or by making cysts, preventing forward movement.

Many women trying to have a child might benefit from considering that impatience works against their bodies' natural wisdom. Asking the ovaries to mature crops of five or more follicles, month after month, is neither natural, nor healthy. The ovaries need to rest; the woman needs to experience stillness and allow recovery. Both are equally important, yet this idea has become foreign in the conception process.

Consider the word "rest" for a moment, as a new action word. "To rest" implies the cessation of movement in order to relax, refresh oneself, or recover strength. Resting is all about waiting, healing, and recharging. However, the average fertility patient tends to equate a rest cycle with failure.

Being overly impatient reveals a woman who is exercising too much of her masculine "yang" energy. By contrast, feminine energy, referred to as "yin" energy, is revealed in a woman who can wait patiently and stay receptive. When we rest, we can get closer to our fertility goal by giving our bodies a chance to recover from being overworked, overtired, and overstimulated.

Imagine an egg cell as she plumps, matures, and ripens in response to rising levels of estrogen. At the right moment, under precise hormonal conditions, her follicle shell will rupture and she is thrust out – to begin the act of floating freely toward the fallopian tube. She has no legs or tail to facilitate movement. She cannot rush anything; she moves only by gravity and the contractions inside the fallopian tube. She relies on both to sufficiently propel her forward, where she may encounter the sperm. In her passivity, the egg is an equally powerful counterpart to the millions of racing sperm in the overall conception process.

Whether doing fertility protocols or trying to conceive naturally, women need to know that a wise egg instinctually *waits for optimal conditions* to ensure safety and create the best possible chance of success. If there is too much adrenaline present in the body, she will halt the process of ovulation and possibly become a cyst to prevent pregnancy. It is all part of our innate design.

Remember: the uterus is a receptacle, and it must also wait for optimal conditions, while staying receptive to the right fertilized embryo. The entire process of fertilization (and pregnancy, as well) is about allowing perfect timing to orchestrate cellular processes that ultimately result in new human beings. In a very profound way, *we become more fertile by being more patient.*

It is perfectly appropriate to be your sperm-like masculine self at work, where that energy tends to be highly valued. But when you come home, try to remind yourself that a key component of your baby-making is your ability to be patient, receptive and open—to your partner or husband, to your own feelings, and to the process itself.

One of my friends is a successful gynecologist/obstetrician. When she and her husband are trying to conceive, she alerts him to her upcoming ovulation by referring to it as "Sexy Time." Using this wording (instead of thinking of it as "timed relations") is one way to help a woman relax and allow nature to prevail, envisioning the buildup to a sexy time, versus something pressurized and scheduled. Do you notice the difference?

My job as a fertility acupuncturist is to help patients cultivate appreciation for all that can happen when we are *slowing down* and being patient. I share what I've learned from how little good results when we race through life, being focused solely on moving from one accomplishment to the next.

Having recovered from an ovarian issue myself, I have incredible respect for the egg and her wisdom. My particular healing process insisted that I cultivate patience *for five years* while my personal conditions ripened appropriately, but my ovaries responded positively as a result.

Grasping this idea of increasing our ability to be patient is vital to getting pregnant, especially when we start later in life. Those precious few eggs that are left to women who are older respond better to far less stimulation and time pressuring. They need more nurturing and a sense of calm in order to mature properly. In the wake of impatience or fear of being too old, however, this common sense logic can easily be forgotten or disregarded.

Chinese medicine acknowledges our human tendency toward

impatience, and therefore includes the practice of T'ai Chi and/or Qi Gong in its healing repertoire. Both practices involve unhurried, steady, balanced movements forward; a true understanding of the essence of being patient. These forms of "moving meditation," help people balance their energy and hormones. Similar to yoga, this ancient practice restores free flow of qi and blood, and emphasizes the importance of breathing, all of which are great for improving fertility odds.

It can be very hard to live at a relaxed pace, continuously trusting and breathing, while the pace of life increases all around us. The truth is, however, that we get so much more out of life when we're in the present moment, appreciating all we have, while patiently waiting for more to be given to us.

Resting Equals Healing

Jessica was a thirty-six-year-old mother of one healthy child, and was having difficulty conceiving her second. She had a job that involved high stress, her days were long and included a challenging commute, and she had a compromised thyroid. Stress had impacted her FSH, which was elevated. There were many obvious factors working against her fertility.

At first she loved coming in for appointments. She was compliant, took herbs, worked less, and rested. She focused on more positive thoughts and started listening to her body, which responded favorably to her slowing down and doing less. Her FSH went down and, as a result, she felt empowered. She told me she believed her eggs were responding to how she was living her life differently and all the new choices she was making.

Ironically, it was these same quick positive results that triggered her to fall back into her deeply entrenched behaviors of impatience and worry. Now that she was feeling better and her FSH had gone down in one short month, she decided to jump back into IVF, viewing it as her best and only option for getting pregnant again. Her doctor confirmed her fears, saying that FSH being elevated *even one time* indicated likely Premature Ovarian Failure, and chances were unlikely she would ever conceive on her own.

It is worth mentioning that this happened to be the same doctor's office I called when my own FSH was elevated initially, when I was thirty-two. In a bit of a panic at that point myself, I called and spoke to a head nurse there. Thinking I was a potential new patient, she explained that when FSH scores were over 20, like mine, the doctor typically advised going straight to an egg donor! That was their recommended scripted answer for people who called asking "that question."

I then disclosed my identity and mentioned how many of this doctor's patients were now at Well Women. I shared how several of the patients had not only lowered their FSH, but some were far into healthy pregnancies. Still others had birthed healthy children already from recovering their infertility naturally. At that point, the head nurse changed her tune completely and said, "Oh yeah, we have seen acupuncture work really well. You *could* try that first."

In Jessica's case, she had been responding favorably to acupuncture, regulating her cycles and improving her lifestyle—until her doctor put the fear of POF back into her mind. She instantly lost her sense of patience and calm, immediately shut down her ovaries with Lupron and birth control pills, and braced herself to prepare for the upcoming IVF cycle.

Feeling desperate, she completely disregarded my previous recommendation to give her body six months of trying naturally. She opted for the fast route, shifted her ovaries into high gear, and put more stress on her already taxed ovaries. I tried to be supportive of her choice, having some understanding of how scared she was, but I was noticeably disappointed in her doctor's decision to cycle her so quickly without much regard for her healing ovaries.

She said she felt guilty about rushing things and felt torn between her two healthcare providers. On the one hand, she said, there was me, her acupuncturist. I was the person who helped her return to herself and feel healthier than she had in years. Then there was her M.D., the person to whom she said she "had given so much money." He, therefore, was the person who might have the more advanced, high-tech, and *immediate* solution.

I really felt for her. The impatience of it all seemed so sad and counter-intuitive. Why would her already depleted body respond favorably to stimulation under such unfavorable conditions? What was the harm in waiting a mere six months to increase the chance of a positive outcome and save her money?

It was no surprise when her body failed to respond to the protocol and her transfer was called off. They didn't have the financial resources to try it again. She was devastated. She did not return for acupuncture, but instead called to tell me she appreciated my help and acknowledged the positive differences the treatments had made.

We found out one year later, through a new patient who knew her, she was actually pregnant, having conceived naturally! She was more than halfway through the pregnancy and doing just fine. It really is wonderful what joys a little time and patience can bring.

My personal opinion with respect to IVF is that it is an *amazing* scientific advancement that gets better every day. Every time fertility doctors cycle a patient, they learn a little more about women's bodies, the miracle of conception, and how to combine the two to make babies. It stands to reason that, as time goes on, these doctors will continue to perfect this procedure, thus increasing the success rate. Just like acupuncture, there most definitely is a place for IVF in the world of infertility. However, for patients who are still in the age range where they can afford to wait just a little longer, they owe it to their bodies to try all things natural first to improve their odds—including but not limited to, being PATIENT!

Chapter 11

Clear Inflammation and Use Food as Fertile Medicine

Until this point, I have presented what I consider the basic spiritual concepts that lay the foundation for improved fertility. The ideas may be new for some, and reminders for others. Either way, when focused upon, those concepts can help you believe that it's possible to heal your infertility on a deeper level and move beyond the "stuck-ness" of infertility.

These next two chapters reveal very specific ways to address your physical body and help you stick it back to infertility with a greater sense of fertile balance. Most fertility patients need to address their diet and lifestyle in order to reach their desired results – because poor choices are often a hidden downfall and source of systemic inflammation that can stand between themselves and their healthy babies.

People frequently overlook the correlation between what they put in their mouths and how those foods will ultimately affect their bodies. An acupuncturist's job is to recognize the existing and potential imbalances in their patients, then educate them with suggestions of how to restore balance and optimize the body as a whole.

The concept of diet-induced inflammation has only recently been recognized and accepted in Western medicine. They now know it is a root cause of several health problems. Defined as "the act of being provoked, roused to anger or hyper-stimulation, resulting in redness, heat, pain or swelling," *inflammation* presents a clear obstacle to getting pregnant.

One powerful way to reduce inflammation within the infertile subculture is to teach the ways that food can be used as "fertile medicine," as there are many foods that are capable of neutralizing chronically inflamed systems.

In the Well Women office, we explain the connection between inflammatory foods and infertility to our patients by describing the interplay between acid and alkaline in the body. "Acid" foods create what is known as pathological heat, and "alkaline" foods clear heat from the system.

Heat-producing, high-acid foods and behaviors include excessive indulgence in the following: sugar, meat protein, alcohol, greasy/spicy food, vinegar salad dressings, chocolate, caffeine, and smoking (cigarettes/ marijuana). In general, these foods and behaviors create stress in the body and increase the body temperature. They create sometimes palpable "hot spots" of inflammation the body has to resolve.

Alkalizing foods, such as dark green leafy vegetables, seaweed, avocado, lemon water, and cucumber, are anti-inflammatory. Considered "cooling" foods, they have the ability to neutralize inflammation and help patients recover their fertility.

With respect to infertility, inflammation speeds up the aging of our gametes, as the heat consumes the "yin essence" and creates an imbalance on a deep level. A woman with a high degree of inflammation needs to work hard to offset the effects of pathological heat, because chronic inflammation reduces the amount of energy she can devote to becoming pregnant and sustaining a healthy pregnancy.

From a physiological standpoint, a woman's body will address chronic inflammation by leaching minerals from the bones. Valuable estrogen stores are compromised to reduce the negative effects of stress hormones (adrenaline and cortisol) and a cascade of inflammatory proteins that are released on a daily basis.

Our reproductive systems eventually weaken from constantly repairing damage caused by inflammatory behaviors. Over time we become less fertile, more vulnerable to infections, more susceptible to autoimmune conditions, and more likely to manifest adhesions that normally present little difficulty for a healthy system to eradicate.

The combination of acidosis, inflammation, and chronic stress leads to a host of fertility obstacles. Inflammation reveals itself most commonly in infertile patients diagnosed with elevated FSH, prematurely aging ovaries, insufficient or hostile cervical mucus, and autoimmune conditions.

Less obviously heat-producing, but just as inflammatory, is the potential damage caused by two seemingly innocuous foods: *glutinous wheat and pasteurized dairy*. Think of the abundance of these highly convenient foods that surround us every day in the form of bagels and cream cheese, muffins, lattes, pizza, sandwich breads, ice cream, cookies, cake, croissants, and countless other comfort foods.

Wheat gluten and pasteurized dairy create an internal environment that generates inflammation indirectly — by first creating "dampness," which obstructs the free flow of energy in the body's system. Excess dampness becomes what is referred to as "phlegm" in Chinese medicine. Phlegm accumulation leads to stagnation, and stagnation typically leads to heat. Imagine a car tire stuck in mud, spinning and creating heat from the friction.

Over time, "phlegm-heat" will create blockages in the reproductive tract, resulting in cysts on the ovaries, fibroids in the uterus, endometriosis/adhesions, polycystic ovarian syndrome, and pelvic inflammatory diseases (PID), in which scar tissue results from longstanding inflammation in or outside the fallopian tubes, rendering them obstructed and potentially useless.

Totally eliminating wheat gluten and pasteurized dairy from the diet is one obvious answer, at least temporarily, to give the body a break from the inflammation cascade. However, letting go of a food we enjoy is not always necessary or easy, so my suggestion is to let readers decide for themselves how seriously to consider the role inflammation plays in their infertility. Based on the degree of your physical symptoms and your individual reproductive issues/goals, you can decide how stringent to be with respect to these food recommendations.

If you choose to keep glutinous wheat and pasteurized dairy in your diet, I suggest eating them in very limited amounts and adding enzyme-rich fermented food (such as cultured vegetables, or unpasteurized sauerkraut) to aid in their digestion. This is especially important if you have endometriosis or autoimmune-related infertility, because gluten and pasteurized dairy greatly aggravate those specific fertility conditions.

For nearly fifteen years I've recommended the *sprouted* form of wheat bread, because the sprouting process of grain allows important enzymes to stay intact that facilitate easier assimilation. Sprouting reduces gut-inflammation and the common side effects of gas, bloating, and cramping typically associated with eating whole-wheat glutinous bread. "Food for Life" is the brand I recommend most frequently, known to many as the "Ezekiel" breads and sprouted grain tortillas. These have a negligible amount of wheat gluten, are easy to find, and taste great.

Contrary to more traditional Chinese medicine practitioners who prescribe a diet consisting of "No Dairy" as their fertility program, I actually recommend highly unpasteurized dairy as a delicious source of calcium, protein, and good fat that can be converted to estrogen to help make better quality eggs. It is particularly beneficial for women who are considered "deficient."

If a woman avoids eating egg yolks and drinks nonfat milk, her body will probably lack sufficient good fat, vitamin D, and cholesterol, and will therefore, need to work harder to create good quality, viable eggs that mature properly and can be fertilized easily. These are women who are generally labeled as "poor responders" or are told they are headed toward premature ovarian failure (POF). My experience has been that these women may only need to augment their diet with whole fat dairy and eggs to improve the number and quality of eggs they produce in their stimulation protocols.

Because raw milk has not been chemically or heat-treated, it retains the enzymes necessary for us to digest it easily, while preventing the scenario of phlegm-heat stagnation. Unpasteurized milk, therefore, allows us to get the healthy benefits *without creating inflammation.* Unpasteurized milk is considered excellent fertile medicine, because its cooling, moistening properties clear heat. Raw milk is alkalizing to our bodies and digests fine in people who are lactose-intolerant!

Briefly review what you ate yesterday. Did you choose "whole foods" such as high quality animal protein, cage-free eggs, organic vegetables and non-GMO seasonal fruit? Or did your menu contain mostly processed food from a box or a restaurant? It may have been convenient and less expensive, but likely it was low in fertile nutrients and high in chemicals that your body will not assimilate well.

It may not be easy to break certain familiar food habits. But it will be worth your trouble to make an attempt to slow down or reverse some of the reproductive damage caused by pathological heat and inflammation. Start by thinking about these past few pages. Be honest: do these suggestions resonate with you, or do they cause anxiety?

"Diet" is a tough word for most people, and so too, is the idea of consuming unpasteurized milk in our Western culture. Find comfort in knowing we all struggle to figure out which foods will best serve our bodies. Know that answers are available, and the information will find a way to those who are ready and open to receive it.

Inflammation is a very real and very common threat to our population. I think it is one of the biggest culprits in many infertility patients' failures to conceive and carry full-term babies. It's at the root of so many undiagnosed physical conditions and warrants consideration as another possible explanation for women who are diagnosed with "unexplained" infertility.

Allowing Food to Heal

Carrie was only thirty when she was referred to our office. She was, like so many patients we treat for infertility, a hard-working, successful, but overtired attorney, with irregular menstrual cycles and a diet consisting of breads and processed frozen entrees. She had a history of abnormal pap smears (what Chinese gynecologists quickly identify as phlegm-heat). Carrie admitted "running on empty." She was overweight and had dark circles under her eyes. Her body ached for rest, but sleep gave very little relief. During the day she was typically cold, suffering from poor circulation, but at night she would sweat like crazy.

Because of her menstrual complaints of pain and irregularity, weight issues, her age and stressful career, I immediately thought of polycystic ovaries, possible endometriosis, and adrenal burnout. I suspected she was relying on sugary foods for the energy and mental sharpness to stay on top of her game. The drops in blood sugar would explain why she was so tired. I explained how erratic swings of blood sugar and reliance on acid foods typically led to the pattern she was experiencing and how she could benefit from the inclusion of more protein, mineral-rich greens, and the exclusion of sugar, wheat, and pasteurized dairy.

Following her first appointment, she started making and eating leafy greens every night and took Chinese herbs I prescribed to reduce her latent heat, phlegm, and inflammation.

The first sign that revealed her body was happier was that her menstrual period returned after a few months' absence. She proceeded to detoxify her system of wheat and sugar, even though it meant having initial fatigue and joint pains from detox. She trusted that her body would appreciate the nutrition eventually, so she kept up the hard work.

She sought the help of a fertility specialist who confirmed my suspicion via ultrasound that her ovaries were surrounded by the phlegm-filled cysts indicative of PCOS. This gave her more trust in me and the way we were approaching her health, motivating her to continue cleaning up her diet. Her doctor found that her husband's sperm morphology was reduced to 2%, an outward example of phlegm-heat in men. His diet, Carrie said, was even worse than hers.

She added a Western glucose-regulating medication known as Metformin to her fertility protocol and I modified her herbs to address the digestive complaints that go with that medication. Carrie continued to stay away from breads and sugary foods, eating something green and leafy every night. We armed her with several wheat alternatives like gluten-free muffins and sprouted bread to use for sandwiches. She fully utilized our office as a resource for useful information, finding more and more relief along the way.

Her doctor wanted to try one stimulated IUI cycle to see how her body would respond. I figured she needed more time to clear phlegm-heat, but supported her decision to go forward. In each appointment, we used the needles to continue clearing inflammation, transform the phlegm congestion in her pelvis, and support her digestion and interest in healthier foods.

Much to everyone's surprise, she conceived healthy twins with that first Clomid-stimulated insemination, demonstrating perfectly how our bodies will respond exactly as they are supposed to when we understand that food, particularly anti-inflammatory food, is fertile medicine.

Chapter 12

Honor the Sun as the Source of All Life

As a fairly new practice, many fertility doctors now prescribe vitamin D supplements as part of their protocols. Including this vital nutrient (that we historically received from exposure to sunshine) in the form of a vitamin pill can be helpful in boosting success rates, but diminishes the role of the sun in nature as the source of life and healing. In fact, a majority of the western medical community would prefer that we avoid the sun's rays at all costs because of the risk of skin cancer.

According to Chinese gynecologists, however, moderate amounts of sunlight (as the source of *yang* energy) can—and should—be included in treating infertility.

Just as insufficient sun in nature causes plants to cease growing, deficient yang and inadequate sun exposure negatively impacts human fertility.

One of the most interesting and powerful revelations Anna and I noticed while creating our "Well Women approach to fertility" was the vast influence sunlight had over women's cycle lengths. This possibility became highlighted as we observed the varied cycle lengths of the women who worked in our office.

The Well Women Acupuncture office is a windowless space. With dark ruby-red carpet, new age trance music streaming, and soft natural lighting, it is a subdued, tranquil healing space. I was often spending ten-twelve hours per day, several days per week, inside this womb-like environment, and the deprivation of sunlight disrupted my cycle length significantly. The lack of light, in addition to the psychological stress I put on myself, had my body ovulating immature follicles only and releasing them too quickly; at one point I was menstruating every twenty-one days. Meanwhile, one office colleague noted that her cycle typically lasted forty-one days, and yet another associate in the office menstruated approximately every thirty-five days.

Studies over the centuries have linked sunlight exposure (and our correlating circadian rhythms) to the timing of our menstruation. Women who spend long periods of time in dark environments ovulate inconsistently.

When our circadian rhythms are thrown off, as it is when we're exposed to long periods of darkness or a lack of natural light, ovulation is thrown off, too. Once I started taking midday, outdoor breaks and spending more time outside on my days off, my body regulated itself and my cycles started lengthening to reflect a more normal twenty-eight-day period.

This raised our awareness about the impact of sunshine and explained the role of "yang" in Chinese medicine, and its ability to affect fertility. Warming the womb, stimulating hormones, rupturing of follicles, protecting implanted embryos, proper timing of various hormone cycles, and virility of the sperm are all functions of sufficient yang in Chinese medicine. Therefore, the sun (as the *source* of yang) plays a bigger role in healthy baby making than we may initially realize.

We all know that the sun is responsible for warming the earth and giving us light. Consider how it also serves as a masculine counterpart to the feminine moon. As the moon governs our menstruation (hence the timing correlation with "lunar cycles"), the sun profoundly influences ovulation.

If we relate the sun and its yang energy to other masculine influences in the body, such as the regulation of certain "yang" sex hormones like testosterone and progesterone, we can suggest that getting a proper amount of sunlight is one effective way to increase or restore many aspects of compromised fertility. Sufficient yang relates to a healthy libido (testosterone influence), while also supporting implantation after ovulation (one role of progesterone).

Men, as well, suffer from reduced levels of sunlight. Vitamin D (typically derived from the sun) is known to be essential for proper development of sperm cells. Vitamin D also improves semen quality and sperm count, and is capable of supporting healthy levels of testosterone.

With our increasingly hectic schedules, it can be difficult to find the time to partake in the healing power of the sun. And when we do indulge, we first apply sunscreens that block the penetration of the sun's rays through our skin. Sunlight deprivation leads to sleep disruption, fatigue, depression, muscle and bone pain. It can also lead to osteoporosis from insufficient vitamin D intake and—most important to those trying to conceive—irregular menstrual timing, sperm issues and ovulatory dysfunction.

In Chinese medicine, yin and yang are said to be inseparable and mutually dependent on one another. We see this in nature with the sun and the moon, each exerting their cyclical effect on our natural reproductive timing. The moon exerts her gravitational pull to influence tidal flow patterns as well as the menstrual flow and cycle lengths of women. Then the sun radiates his light to regulate rupturing and growth of "seeds" and the timing of ovulation. Human beings have an inseparable relationship with circadian rhythms (the fluctuating periods of sunlight and darkness) and it greatly influences our fertility.

Understanding the four phases of the menstrual cycle according to Chinese gynecology and what's happening at each phase will further explain why the warming "yang" phase that follows ovulation is so important. Chinese gynecology attributes the first seven days of a woman's cycle to what is referred to as "blood." The woman is bleeding and her hormones are at their lowest. As her lining is being shed, she is, in effect, cleansing.

From day seven until ovulation occurs, "yin" is the focal point of the cycle. This is known as the estrogenic, follicular phase leading up to ovulation that is focused solely on the development of the follicle that houses a maturing egg. From ovulation and for 7 days following, "yang" is emphasized in the menstrual cycle as the warming aspect of the luteal phase. Sufficient yang triggers the process of ovulation, the actual rupture and release of the egg. An abundance of yang in the woman's body is then responsible for keeping progesterone levels increased (progesterone is thermogenic, and thus warms the body) to support implantation and sustain pregnancy.

The final week of the menstrual cycle (a premenstrual phase which begins one-week *post*-ovulation and lasts until bleeding begins) correlates with the proper flow of qi through the body. If the woman's energy is properly balanced, and the other three vital substances (blood, yin and yang) are sufficient, the qi will flow freely for seven days until bleeding begins. If fertilization and implantation occur, the body's qi will then be used to facilitate proper division of embryonic cells into a fetus.

It is at mid-cycle, somewhere between cycle days 11-16, that yang energy exerts its greatest influence. In Chinese gynecology, the LH surge represents a "transformation of *yin into yang*." This eloquently describes how yin, *a substance* (sufficient estrogen to mature the follicle), will promote yang, *the action* (rupturing of the egg from the follicle) as the two parts work together to facilitate successful ovulation.

There must be sufficient yin and yang for the process of ovulation to occur. At mid-cycle there must also be a sudden increase, or surge, in yang to catalyze the entire reaction. This surge of yang energy triggers the release of the egg from the follicle, and promotes its movement down the fallopian tube.

Deficiencies of yang energy reveal themselves in women who benefit from Clomid use (a medication taken to promote ovulation). Clomid is taken prior to ovulation and has a side effect of warming the body in the luteal phase, sometimes drying vaginal fluids. We would say, from the Chinese gynecology standpoint, that Clomid can assist yang-deficient women by warming their yang energy to help trigger the mid-cycle transformation. Women with yang deficiency have a hard time conceiving and sustaining pregnancy.

Chinese doctors treating infertility will recommend warm meat-based soups, warming foods and spices after ovulation to support implantation. Foods like lamb, beef, or chicken, and herbs such as turmeric, ginger, fennel, and cinnamon are examples of foods that supplement yang. Acupuncturists specializing in fertility also insist patients wear socks to bed and slippers around the house to prevent their feet from transferring cold up into the womb.

A "cold womb" results from insufficient yang and constant consumption of cold foods, as well as being improperly dressed in cold environments. Think ice cream, icy fruit smoothies, iced drinks in general, swimming in cooler Autumn and Winter months, wearing flip-flops and short skirts when it is cold outside or during our menstrual period. All of these behaviors allow cold to travel from our unprotected feet upwards along the conception channels, thus bringing cold into the womb.

Conversely, exposing your hands, legs, arms, and face (without sunscreen) to only *a few minutes* of sunlight twice a week and for an hour or so on cycle days thirteen and fourteen (regardless of the length of your current cycle pattern) can surprisingly help correct a mild case of improperly timed ovulation and cycle length irregularities.

Sunshine, vitamin D (2000-5000IU/day), socks, and warmer food choices after ovulation will increase your body's yang and give your brain a sense of warmth. Applying hot packs to your low abdomen and low back around ovulation (if you notice these areas prefer warmth, or if you tend to run cold) also increases yang energy. Furthermore, doing these things will soothe and relax your body—all good when you are trying to conceive.

Sunshine Restores Diminished Yang Qi

Morgan was a prior patient who returned to work with me for help with a second healthy pregnancy. She had a miscarriage before conceiving her son, and that was what had led her to meet me in the first place a few years prior. When we worked together initially we learned that she was progesterone deficient (considered a form of yang deficiency). So she had previously supplemented with oral progesterone.

While trying for her second child, Morgan miscarried again. After this second miscarriage and finding out her FSH was elevated at 13.1, her doctor told her that she should prepare to go straight to IVF. She was only thirty-three, but supposedly she was "headed for Premature Ovarian Failure."

Morgan wasn't sleeping well and neither was her son, who was being transitioned into a "big boy" bed. Her cycles were very short (twenty-four days or less). She was exhausted from overworking and attempting to be a perfect wife, mother, housekeeper, and first grade teacher. She wanted a second opinion about her eggs, so I recommended one of the MDs I work with regularly, and we began optimizing her mind and body to bring in baby number two.

During the first month of treatment, we focused solely on getting her to relax in an attempt to lower her FSH. The needles worked their magic and her FSH was immediately reduced from 13.1 to 8.3. Her cycle lengthened by two days. She was happy seeing these positive results and felt more at peace. Because she had a history of working successfully with me, Morgan was very compliant with my instructions and took her herbs faithfully.

Due to her known low levels of progesterone, I was able to diagnose yang deficiency again. I looked for other ways to warm her and hopefully lengthen her luteal phase even more. When her next cycle started, it was summertime, so I suggested she take her son to the beach for a few hours on Days thirteen and fourteen. This would reset both of their Circadian clocks in an attempt to improve their sleeping problems and lengthen her cycle by yet another day.

She was surprised how her sleep was restored immediately. After ovulation we watched as her twenty-three-day cycle made it to twenty-five days, then twenty-seven days. On day thirty, she allowed herself to take a home test, and found it positive! Again, she supplemented with progesterone, continued with acupuncture for nausea and fatigue, and now has two little boys!

Sometimes it really can be this simple. Contrary to what the science may suggest from lab values, keep in mind that women's bodies are programmed to procreate. Nature can surprise us... when we employ some of its most basic remedies.

Part 2

Look Beyond Your "Infertile" Diagnosis

Chapter 13

Be Willing to Make Changes

Being willing to change your life to improve your fertility is key to your success; the willingness to stretch beyond your comfort zone allows for important personal growth. For some, this means beginning a holistic form of treatment that may include yoga, meditation, acupuncture, and/or herbs. Others may need to be willing to make more drastic life changes to get to baby, such as moving, changing jobs or partners, or putting an end to an old habit.

True willingness will require you to actively participate in some form of physical and spiritual transformation. Choosing to become a willing participant in your life is the best way I know for women to improve their chances of becoming mothers. Similarly, this willingness to change that which no longer works for us determines our likeliness of getting everything else we want from life.

Perhaps your recollection of the family-building experience has included only what you perceive as disappointment, frustration, sadness, frequent doctors' appointments, and expensive treatments. If so, then you must be willing to commit yourself 100% to changing those thoughts. Begin to allow more fertile consciousness to stream through your brain instead. Whenever the old thoughts of hopelessness enter your mind, you must be willing to *reframe* them into something more in alignment with your desire and life purpose.

As I have described, my own path appeared to be fraught with fertility challenges. However, honest self-evaluation revealed that my biggest fertility impediment was actually a subconscious unwillingness to embrace a "master plan" that was trying to unfold in my life. I had made so many changes to my life in terms of diet, lifestyle, and my way of thinking that I thought I was demonstrating a strong willingness to do whatever was necessary to get to baby. Yet, I continued wasting time in relationships with men who had no interest in partnership, commitment, or family building.

I repeatedly tried to manifest a courtship that mimicked what I saw consistently in the lives of my friends and patients. It would naturally be something traditional and conventional. The relationship would develop in a "linear" fashion, along the lines of dating for a few years, followed by one year of engagement. We'd have a nice wedding and then, *together* we would decide how to attempt to have children. I invested a great amount of energy into trying to create that reality for myself, not realizing that in doing so I was actually stopping the flow of what was trying to come to me!

Three different times between ages thirty-three and thirty-six, I found myself heartbroken by men who, merely days earlier, had talked of making a commitment to me. After several months of dating, each of these men ended our relationships without warning. All three of these men left following the honest conversations in which I revealed that I felt ready to test out my efforts to improve my fertility, and possibly start a family.

These situations felt unfair and heart wrenching at the time. They seemed to say to me, *you are not meant to have kids.* But in reality, I was being asked to be willing to let go of my attachments to the conventional mindset about how my life was to unfold.

Much like having three pregnancies that surprisingly led to miscarriage, three times over I experienced the loss of my romantic dream of getting married before a certain age, and all that comes with the traditional expectation of marriage. Like unexplained habitual loss, no one could offer a reason why this was happening.

I felt powerless over the situation that had me repeatedly questioning my life's unfolding and wondering if I really was destined to not have a partner and children. I think most women would have thought the same. Luckily, I had matured enough from years of counseling to know that at least I was in control of how I chose to let the losses affect me. After the third unexpected break up, I gave in to the process. I surrendered.

Instead of returning to the dating world, I picked up a pen and began writing about my experiences and the many triumphs that had emerged inside the office, working with such amazing patients. This was my way of telling Spirit that I was finally willing to use my gift of communication to inspire even more women, by means of creating this book, something I had been talking about doing for years.

The biggest turning point in my infertility adventure came with the writing of this chapter about willingness; as that was the moment when I realized that I needed to be willing to love the life that was meant for me. I needed to be willing to embrace and revel in how different it looked from what everyone else had, instead of feeling sad about what was not there. I was helping women do what science had told them was impossible…and that was worth celebrating!

As a result, I could trust that I wouldn't be left behind, and began considering alternative options. I entertained the prospect of using donor eggs, and at one point I considered fostering troubled teens. In these moments of deep introspection, I actually visualized both as a likely future for myself.

As I wrote more about willingness, I concluded that passing on the predisposition towards endometriosis might not be such a good idea after all. I thought, "Maybe a baby from donor eggs is how I am meant to raise a healthy child." I went further with that feeling and realized, "If I am willing to love any baby that comes to me, not just those who carry my genes, then I can relax around this. Instead of worrying that time is running out, I can focus on how I will someday pay for donor eggs."

I continued this train of thought about willingness and concluded that

I was *not* willing to be a single mom because of my stressful upbringing, as well as my devotion to my life's work and the long hours it entails. I allowed this "unwillingness" to be a healthy boundary for myself. However, this conclusion meant that I would need to be willing to trust life to bring me a man who was not only available, but also accepting of the idea that we may have a child that was not half me. And, on some level, he'd need to be able to accept that I was already married... to my work.

Here was an opportunity for true spiritual transformation. I was struck at my core as I realized that being willing to change, to allow, to reframe and to view things differently, was one empowering way to feel somewhat in control of my destiny.

Willingness is a state of mind; it is what we reveal when we consciously invite change into our lives and *let it happen*. To have the opportunity to start a family, I would need to be open and willing to let it come to me in a different form than I had always imagined. I'd need to actively practice the spiritual concepts that I had shared with my patients for years. If I allowed this purely spiritual aspect of healing to emerge and move through me, then I'd be much more likely to become one of the many success stories to emerge from the Well Women office!

Are you willing to apply these spiritual concepts and practices to create a better life for yourself? Are you willing to be patient, to find more faith, to let go of toxic thoughts and behaviors? Can you trust that your life is unfolding in a most perfectly intended way, even if it's not what you had ever imagined?

Ready and Willing to Be Her Best Self

When I began offering lectures about the ways acupuncture can improve fertility, a woman named Sharon showed up at one of our events. Sharon became quite practiced at being negative about life in general. During my presentation one evening, Sharon sat the farthest away and watched me very closely. As I used the analogy of "a journey" to describe the path to pregnancy, I could sense her trying hard not to roll her eyes. But she listened patiently and took copious notes, especially when I gave specific information about what foods infertile women should eat, and why. Despite seeming put-off by my "spiritual" approach to motherhood, I had a feeling she would eventually find her way to my office. About six months later she did.

Sharon came in saying she had switched from her previous acupuncturist, feeling there was some truth to what I had said at the lecture. She wanted some spiritual help to get beyond her infertile status. I was impressed then, finding nothing more attractive than a woman's willingness to reveal her emotional vulnerability. Her honest acknowledgment that a transformation was necessary validated why I do this work.

By the time Sharon had made her appointment, her transformation into a more willing personality with a more loving spirit was well underway. She had decided to use a donor's eggs, which proclaimed to the universe that she was willing to release the attachment to the idea that her child must be genetically hers.

During her acupuncture sessions she disclosed several stories revealing a conflicted past. I kept directing her to focus on the present moment and all the blessings she had to feel grateful for, being unwilling to let her go back to memories that had already haunted her for almost an entire lifetime.

Our few weeks together passed quickly and soon it was time for her embryo transfer. I met her at the transfer site to do acupuncture to help her relax and completely surrender those old angry attachments to the past.

In that intense moment in her cycle, the physical and emotional culmination point of all her efforts, I asked her to imagine a future in which she could have everything she desired. I stated that it could be hers if only she'd be willing to let go of the angry persona she used to cope with her pain and disappointment.

What happened next caught me by surprise. She shouted out, "I don't want to be that person anymore!" Then she started loudly sobbing. Between the unstoppable waves of tears, she unraveled a list of behavioral traits she was willing to give up that she had come to hate about herself. She declared she was willing to release this self-sabotaging behavior and the negative qualities she said she was unaware of until then.

In that moment, everything was lined up perfectly for a tremendous release. And release, she did! Her willingness was palpable, and it was powerful enough to help her conceive, finally, on that Sunday morning, after *years* of unsuccessful, frustrating attempts. Her new willingness to be a softer person gave her a beautiful daughter to love with the same intensity she revealed that day.

One year later Sharon stopped in to introduce the baby to me. Her face was still completely free of the pain and anger that had once made her look mad all the time. She looked much more at ease, demonstrating that she had maintained her willingness to let happiness replace years of pain.

Chapter 14

Create a Fertile Garden

Imagining the uterus as a potential "fertile garden" can help women overcome infertility. If we reflect upon what makes a garden capable of growing flowers, fruits, or vegetables, we already have an appreciation for the hard work that goes into it. There's an easy understanding that certain requirements must be met for *any* garden to be successful.

We know that a combination of wisdom, detachment, and trusting is what it takes to see planted seeds begin to sprout, so we don't try to control the magic of nature's divine plan. In regards to a garden, we're able to let the process unfold, without much overthinking or worry. An experienced gardener relies on his or her knowledge of seasons, natural cycles, and proper timing in order to increase the likelihood of harvesting a fruitful crop. Just as important are proper weeding techniques, sufficient sunlight, healthy seeds, and adequately nourished soil.

Women who can see themselves as gardeners become more proactive in their fertility process and get excited when they can take matters into their own hands. These women play an active role in recovering their fertility, because not only does the chance for a positive result increase, but they feel more in control of their outcome. Therefore, they tend to be less anxious throughout the process.

Patients who became successful parents have told me that when they applied the words "weeding and nurturing" to the process of resolving infertility, it felt more likely that they would overcome the odds stacked against them. They understood that they were ultimately the ones in charge of pulling their emotional weeds and nurturing their tiny seeds. They felt empowered once more.

Imagine your own uterine lining. Is this "soil" the proper texture, free of clumps, clots, and dry, cracked clay? Is it adequately hydrated and nourished with fresh blood and minerals from your diet and lifestyle?

Allow yourself to entertain the idea that unprocessed emotional wounds can harm your fertile soil just as opportunistic, pathological weeds would take over your backyard. Does it make sense to you that resolving those old, conflicted emotions might have the potential to remove subconscious barriers to fertility?

Would you agree that *positive thoughts* are the seeds you want growing in your garden? Have you cultivated enough spiritual light and understanding to shine on your seeds and help them become capable of making their own healthy seeds someday?

For years, I've successfully used these metaphors and posed these questions to the women who come into the office or participate in my fertility workshops. It helps them gain perspective about how to cultivate the most optimal conditions for their fertile garden. Whether they are determined to have their own children, or welcome children via adoption or otherwise, these concepts can prepare women in such a powerful way.

Frequently, couples renovate their space or move to new homes in order to create sufficient room for baby; or we see them make huge adjustments to their work schedules and lifestyles, changing patterns in their relationships with others, reconciling their emotions, and receiving acupuncture on a regular basis. All of this behavior can be viewed as tilling the soil—breaking things up to allow for fresh growth. They take our individual diet suggestions seriously, and may take herbal prescriptions as part of the nurturing aspect of preparing their garden. They incorporate useful psychological tools to help them pull the emotional weeds, so that healthy life can grow inside their bodies.

Fibroids, endometriosis, scant menstrual periods, or severe hemorrhaging each month are some indications that your garden needs tending. For the most optimal outcome, it's in your best interest to invest some time and energy looking at these issues before engaging in yet another assisted cycle, or prior to beginning the process of ART and IVF.

Tending to Ourselves First

Teresa was thirty-nine-years-old when she was referred to the Well Women office. She had one previous miscarriage, as well as a pregnancy that was terminated after amniocentesis revealed Down's syndrome at week sixteen.

Married for nearly twenty years already, this couple had very established routines and behavioral patterns. Teresa had a pattern of stressing out about work and life in general, and Tim, her husband, consistently provided humor to lessen the impact of her mood swings and resulting insults.

Early in her treatment, we changed her diet to incorporate a more nutritious breakfast that included more protein. We substituted healthier afternoon snacks that were beneficial. Right away she started feeling better and less irritable. Teresa was much happier and more relaxed at work. She said everyone noticed and commented on the change in her demeanor.

It was not surprising that she conceived fairly soon into her course of treatment. But sadly, this pregnancy resulted in another miscarriage. A simple diet change was not enough to prepare an adequately fertile garden that could grow a healthy child. Teresa and Tim took a break from acupuncture, returning a year later after much had shifted for them.

One of the most significant changes I noticed was Teresa's improved relationship with Tim's mother. After nearly two decades, it appeared these two women had resolved some unspoken issues with each other. There had always been a feeling of disappointment wedged between them that Teresa presumed was the result of having produced no grandchildren.

Teresa described large family events in which she felt a subtle emphasis on her childlessness.

A huge shift occurred for this couple when they purchased a piece of family-owned property. At last, they were homeowners, able to leave apartment life behind them. Having lived in an apartment all her life, Teresa admitted she unconsciously placed a significant amount of value on raising children in a house with a yard, because she missed out on that experience herself.

This house represented so much for these two that they appeared giddy with excitement. They told me how they planted a garden, were enjoying entertaining family, and said they felt grounded in a way they never had before. They felt settled enough to *grow roots* of their own. Teresa shared that several grandchildren had been conceived in that house, and said it was built on very fertile land.

One day soon after, she appeared at the office wearing a beautiful ring given to her by her mother-in-law! The ring symbolized healing between the two women. Ironically, it was composed of 3 interconnected circles, which I suggested resembled a healthy egg inside a follicle, inside the ovary. I asked her to think of the ring as a fertility aid. Every time she looked at it, she was instructed to imagine that her ovaries could still produce brilliantly healthy eggs.

More than twenty years after they said, "I do," this couple was proud to host their first large family Thanksgiving dinner in their new home—indulging in a bounty of vegetables Tim had grown in their fertile garden. He was so proud.

When Teresa came in the following week for treatment, she reported that Thanksgiving was "absolutely perfect." Tim's turkey recipe was a masterpiece, the garden's vegetables were perfectly ripe, the house was welcoming, and the company was wonderful. None of it could have been better.

"And to top it off," she revealed, "I ovulated that night!"

After eleven years of trying to conceive a healthy baby, Teresa and Tim had finally cultivated a real-life garden, as well as a metaphorical fertile garden, and conceived their daughter on Thanksgiving night. The inner personal work she had done, and her ability to make significant life changes, helped her have one of the happiest pregnancies I have ever seen.

Chapter 15

Commit to a More Positive Outlook

One of the questions we have on our new patient questionnaire is "What do you think holds you back from having a healthy pregnancy?" Asking this question directly at the onset of treatment is the best way for me to assess a woman's attitude about actualizing motherhood.

To determine where *you* stand, close your eyes, take a deep breath, and ask yourself what you honestly believe will be your fated outcome.

Right away, one of two things will happen. Either a feeling of certainty and positive expectation will fill you; or anger, frustration, and sadness will start to rise up, as negative thoughts take over.

It's fine to be in either place, but there is a catch. Whatever you think, feel and believe... is *exactly what you will continue to create*.

There is a clear reason for this: Your energy follows your thought process. Whatever you are thinking sends your energy in that direction. Negative thoughts generate negative outcomes, and positive thoughts impact yourself and others positively. Cultivating positivity is so simple to understand, yet requires constant attention and practice in order to maintain and master. It can feel awkward and almost foreign at first, but the resulting good feelings that come from having a more positive attitude make it worth the trouble of learning this new practice.

For example, entertaining thoughts such as: "Things always work out for me," "I have a lot of support in my life," or "I always attract loving people to me," practically guarantees those outcomes. With respect to infertility, if you constantly say things like: "I don't think it's going to work," "It's never going to happen," "My eggs are bad and I'm a poor responder," it's likely that pregnancy and motherhood will continue to elude you.

Staying aware of our thoughts is empowering, and therefore important if we are pursuing healthy pregnancy. Reminder messages to remain positive in the midst of uncertainty appear everywhere we look these days. Notice all the inspirational books on the shelves and inspiring messages posted on the Internet. Look at how many workshops are available to help us get a grip on those negative thoughts!

Understanding the Mind-Body connection and the need to stay positive is not just a New Age trend. It is a way of living consciously and in a state of abundance. Negative thinking can prevent us from having what we want and deserve.

Every one of us experiences frustration, disappointment, and uncertainty. After all, life sticks it to us, sometimes daily. Yet, some people steadily maintain their positive outlook, regardless of negative circumstances. They are consistently able to reframe the conditions that appear to be negative, in order keep their spirit light, despite disappointment, loss, and transitions.

Becoming more positive starts with the decision to listen more closely to what you are telling yourself and others. Ask yourself now, "What percent of the time am I undermining my fertility success by thinking defeating, negative, angry thoughts?" Then ask, "How much of my fertility focus is infused with positive thoughts or affirmations that subconsciously confirm my success?"

Start observing yourself closely today. Increase your awareness of negativity and note when it creeps in. Recall who you spent time with during the week... Are these people contributing positively to your life? Or are you surrounding yourself with people who bring you down with their negative mindsets and fears? Do you feel energized after talking with friends and family, or drained, exhausted and/or sick when you have to be around certain people?

After you assess how frequently you create negative thought patterns, you may realize that you have created a habit of resorting to negativity, or have subconsciously become "addicted" to feeling unhappy.

Research scientist Candace Pert, Ph. D., has published a significant amount of information explaining our physiological dependence on the feelings that are generated by our thought patterns. Her book, *Molecules of Emotion,* explains the science behind how we become addicted to certain feelings and literally poisoned by others.

As we feel sadness, pain, love, worry, and anger, different corresponding substances are released into the body that modify its cellular machinery. This explains how our thoughts "make" us sick or sub-fertile, and reveals why positive lifestyle choices such as endorphin-releasing acupuncture treatments and time spent with positive-minded people is so powerful.

We know now that cells have *opiate receptors* that allow our body to process endorphins in response to acupuncture, sexual orgasm, or from strongly focusing our thoughts on something we perceive to be really good. The more often we circulate endorphins in our bloodstream, the more practiced we become at feeling good.

Acupuncture accesses these opiate receptors and consistently causes the body to fully relax. Subsequently, it's an incredibly effective healing modality. In the case of infertility, where so much emotional tension arises from feelings of disappointment, grief, and loss, acupuncture's relaxation properties are incredibly beneficial. Each session provides women with an opportunity to diffuse their painful feelings and *restore their positive outlook.*

Even without acupuncture, we can create the same good feelings simply by taking our thoughts out to our desired outcome. Feel those desires achieved already. Feel yourself with a healthy child already. The process will allow your energy to begin flowing in that direction.

If you combine the benefits of acupuncture with spiritual awareness, supportive friends, and a serious commitment to having a more positive attitude, you will significantly increase your chance of a healthy outcome. At the very least, you'll drastically improve your quality of life and your attitude about what happens in it each day.

Possibility Thinking Makes a Huge Difference

Sharon's doctor sent her to me right before her IVF embryo transfer date. She called wanting to make arrangements for acupuncture on the day of transfer only, since she lived almost 2 hours away from the office. I explained that my preference was to first meet at the office at least once before her transfer. My associates and I prefer to have the chance to get a sense of any possible pattern of disharmony in advance of the patient's transfer day, so that we can assess what holds her back, and offer more personalized care at that very important moment in her cycle.

In Sharon's case, I learned that infertility had been a problem for years already. She was thirty-five at her first appointment, but two years prior they had adopted their son after dozens of natural cycles and IVF treatments had failed. They chose adoption back then, agreeing that the urge to be parents was stronger than the need to experience pregnancy. Now they wanted to try to give him a sibling and were resorting back to IVF.

She agreed to drive in for her initial acupuncture appointment to give me the best chance to help her. At the appointment she informed me how important it was for her not to get her hopes up. Sharon explained how she never allowed herself to spend much time thinking about the process actually working. Intrigued, I asked her how she decided this ambivalent way of thinking was the best course of action.

She thought about it and announced proudly, "My Dad. He always told us never to expect anything. That way we would never be disappointed. If we aren't optimistic, we won't ever have to feel sad if things don't work out. We're already prepared for the bad news!"

"Yikes! Does that belief system serve him well? Has that way of thinking worked for him? Is he never disappointed?" I asked her. I was completely bewildered and yet impressed that she could explain so matter-of-factly such a pathological, family-rooted belief.

We both paused until she said, "No, actually. He *NEVER* gets anything he wants. He is the unhappiest person I know."

Her own words shocked her. I was excited! *Right there* was the reason we needed to work together in advance. Never would I be able to get her attention focused on something this huge inside one of the MD's transfer sites. She would be too distracted with the buzz of the medical office and the anticipation of receiving her embryos.

Sharon needed to have someone shake up her old beliefs and show her that those negative, limiting beliefs belonged to someone else. *She* could start in that very moment to be positive. It certainly couldn't hurt! Would it be so terrible to think IVF just might work for them?

She returned a few days later, with more reason to be negative. Tests revealed that the DNA inside her husband's sperm was fragmented by more than 50%. They would need to supplement their IVF protocol with donor sperm as a backup plan for fertilization. They'd have to take the chance that her husband's sperm would actually be the ones with DNA capable of fertilizing her eggs.

Despite this new and potentially devastating news, Sharon was really optimistic. She smiled and refused to attach negativity to the prognosis. She was doing a good job of keeping her hopes up now, even though it was new for her.

Sharon received acupuncture, staying calm and positive, while across town her eggs were selecting her husband's sperm cells over the donor's!

Sharon ultimately ended up with four fertilized embryos that looked good; she got two embryos fertilized by each man's sperm. As the day went on, the embryos fertilized by the sperm donor failed to progress. They stopped dividing, and the embryos fertilized by her husband continued to look good.

I pointed out that there was something sweet here to be grateful for, and suggested that she try to stay as positive as possible.

These two embryos, the embodiment of the love shared between these two people wanting a brother for their adopted son, were implanted.

She conceived and had a successful pregnancy!

Two years later she returned for another "mental tune-up" because they were going through IVF again. Her husband had used various supplements and made lifestyle changes, greatly improving his sperm quality. They had always dreamed about having a large family.

Sharon said she needed a stronger reminder to be positive this time around because now the pressure was really on them to pull it off again. I understood, but reminded her of the lesson that came from the previous pregnancy—to simply stay open to the possibility of it working out. I asked her to remember that despite all the odds, and in the presence of presumably more virile donated sperm, their own cells had bonded and made a child once before. It *could* happen again.

At this, she smiled. Sharon found out two weeks later she had conceived. This cycle yielded another healthy son! Nine months after his birth, I saw her for one last round of acupuncture before she started what would be her final IVF cycle. Her dream of having a large family was about to be fulfilled.

For a third time she combined acupuncture, positive thoughts, love for her life with her husband and sons, and IVF. The combination resulted in the birth of a baby girl, and more joy in her life than she could have ever imagined.

Chapter 16

Visualize Yourself as a Mother

Relatively few people choose to develop their gift of insight, to see beyond fear and negativity. Previous disappointment can make it hard to believe that we possess the power to manifest what we have always seen for ourselves. However, my experience has been that infertile women's hearts are *comforted* when they give themselves permission to look beyond their infertile diagnosis, and visualize having a healthy baby.

We constantly get mental glimpses of things that could be coming our way. These images present quickly as flashes, snapshots, or symbols in our mind's eye. Or we may just have a "knowing" about something. Often we brush these thought forms away, having been taught to disregard them as daydreams or fantasies.

These sensory perceptions are nothing to fear or downplay in significance. They are actually signs and symbols representing *possibilities* that might exist in our future.

When we begin to trust these images, we can allow ourselves to see them as potential realities for our lives. Then we can entertain the thought that every move we make and everything that happens in our lives is bringing us closer to what we've seen in those snapshots.

The power to see and tap into this knowingness is within each of us. In exchange for bringing our visions into reality, we have to *stay open to receiving insights*. When we have an open mind we can consciously allow our sensory and visual powers to be strengthened, being made even more accurate over time. Meanwhile, we make conscious efforts to allow the energetic shifts that may be necessary to create the right conditions for what we've seen.

My associates and I help women visualize themselves as mothers. We help them trust the glimpses they may have seen. We help them recognize possible sensory clues that they may not have perceived on their own. We start by asking if they can see a family for themselves, or if they've always had a feeling they would have a family. If they say yes, we hold that space for them, supporting them as they develop more of a detailed image for themselves. Believing that they will achieve what they have visualized for years helps calm their anxiety and restore their faith.

"What's important," I emphasize, "is that you can see kids as a part of your future. Knowing *how* you get to them, and what is involved in their path, may not be as clear. Your ability to see them implies that the *possibility* of motherhood exists for you."

We often start each acupuncture treatment with a guided meditation, or by providing positive images for the patients to consider while resting with the needles. Our words help them envision themselves with healthy reproductive tracts, fertile eggs, a swollen belly, and an easy pregnancy. We may suggest they visualize a picture of themselves holding a healthy baby in their arms and just imagine that reality for a moment, even though it has not yet been actualized.

As the women become more familiar with this language and practice of visualization, they begin to feel more comfortable practicing it on their own. Being able to visualize holding a child can offer some reassurance when nothing else seems to quell the growing doubts and fears.

If you can see a baby, but he or she has not yet appeared, it's likely that other aspects of your life require your attention first, in order to create the proper conditions. Use your creative visualization skills to "look inside" and see what obstacles may be blocking forward movement along your path to motherhood. Then visualize yourself moving beyond the perceived obstacle.

Patty Always Saw Two

At almost forty-years-old, Patty arrived at the Well Women Acupuncture office after seeing our website. Despite her age, her FSH was only 4.8 and her estradiol level was fine at 48 points. Her husband's sperm had some compromised motility, but pregnancy was a likely outcome for this couple. Insemination and Clomid seemed like a winning formula. In fact, when I met Patty, she was anxious that she had responded too well to Clomid, because she produced five follicles. She was nervous about the possibility of twins.

"I've always seen two kids for myself, Danica," she said with some trepidation. "I just know I'm gonna have two, probably twins, and I'm so excited and nervous at the same time!" I found her unwavering confidence in her vision refreshing, because so many other women need us to help them find it. But here was Patty, not just sure she would get pregnant, but positive she would have two. It was inspiring.

The Clomid with IUI protocol worked for her, and she conceived immediately. But soon after, she started becoming anxious.

"I just know there are two," she insisted, and I was inclined to believe her, she was so convincing.

When her first ultrasound revealed only one sac and one heartbeat, she was confused. Not disappointed, not sad, just very, very confused.

"I could swear there were two spirits inside of me, maybe one of them didn't make it," she said before resting with the needles.

Her pregnancy continued for about six more weeks; all the while she was increasingly uncomfortable. She had cramps and indigestion, and tremendous anxiety that something was wrong inside. I recall that she had to resort to taking Klonopin to calm her nerves. This type of extraordinary, off-the-charts level of anxiety when the pregnancy is otherwise progressing normally often indicates a woman is carrying a nonviable fetus with an impending miscarriage.

A few weeks later, Patty insisted on a CVS (Chorionic Villi Sampling) diagnostic procedure. She could not shake the feeling that there was something wrong with her growing baby.

It turned out that she was right on several levels. Something was not right with her baby, and there was the possibility that, at one time, there actually were two spirits inside her womb.

Her fetus was confirmed to have Kleinfelter's Syndrome, which meant she was carrying a boy with an extra female X chromosome; he appeared as XXY in the screening test. Were two embryos created that merged into one somehow, she wondered, or did her implanted embryo have this genetic problem from the beginning? After much analysis, she concluded that continuing the pregnancy was not in the child's best interest.

A few months passed. Another pregnancy from stimulated IUI also ended in miscarriage. Patty entered a period of depression that was combined with weight gain and high blood pressure. She was having a hard time resisting the emotional urge to eat, and resorted to isolating herself, feeling so confused inside. How could she see two kids so clearly and have such trouble getting to them?

Patty and her husband took a few extended tropical vacations. They spent time talking about their situation, and they also took a break from thinking about starting a family. Patty took time to heal before returning to the confident place she had once been, where it was okay to see herself as a mother of two.

When she was ready to do so, she returned to the Well Women office. She said the treatments and the energy of our staff had always been instrumental in helping her get grounded and made her feel calmer. She also had some big news. The couple opted to take a completely different course to get to their kids. Patty explained that they had already picked an egg donor *and* a surrogate.

The first surrogate she picked got pregnant right before Patty's donor cycle was to begin. But she maintained her steadfast determination to "see" this vision of her family all the way through to the end.

She found another surrogate. Patty and her new surrogate, Tina, hit it off very well. The two developed a quick friendship that was rooted in the faith that they were brought together for a distinct purpose. The chemistry between the two of them was undeniable, as I witnessed at the time of the embryo transfer. The three of us discussed the various twists and turns that had been involved in Patty's quest to be a mom.

It seemed that the combination of a twenty-three-year-old donor and a twenty-three-year-old surrogate was destined to be her route to motherhood. *That* was the part of her vision that was not revealed to her. That, apparently, was the missing piece to this puzzle.

After the transfer, Patty, her husband, her surrogate, and I all waited to see what would become of the two embryos transferred into Tina's uterus. Very early, Tina exhibited several pregnancy symptoms. Patty maintained her faith in her vision, stating clearly that she "just knew" that she and her husband were going to raise twins as she had seen all along.

Very elevated blood levels of fetal hormone confirmed Patty's suspicion of a multiple pregnancy. Anxiety soared high during the time between the bloodwork and the first ultrasound. Nine days later, ultrasound confirmed there were indeed two sacs, and two healthy heartbeats! Thirty-eight weeks later, Patty and her husband welcomed their two babies into their family just as she had always envisioned.

Chapter 17

Set Clear Boundaries

Whenever I mention to a patient that she needs to "set some boundaries," the response is almost always a groan of resignation. Being truthful with others about where our boundaries lie is scary sometimes. Telling people honestly what you think or feel is likely to create some uncomfortable moments. However, tremendous freedom and peace come from establishing boundaries with the people in our lives. Properly doing so can help you have more energy to improve your fertility.

Enforcing clear boundaries with other people is important to fertility because doing so helps maintain the integrity of a woman's immune system and nervous system, and decreases unnecessary emotional stress. Poor boundaries with co-workers, friends, or family result in situations where a woman does more than what is physically or emotionally reasonable for her to do. Sometimes, she may even feel forced to do things against her will. This scenario can put a significant stress on her body and may eventually affect her reproductive capacity.

It was my personal experience with endometriosis and having over 200 adhesions surgically removed from my pelvic cavity that revealed to me the correlation between this disease and my lack of boundaries with certain people. I routinely said yes to people in my life, even when I knew I that saying no was more in my best interest.

Some examples of how we may have lost sight of our physical and emotional boundaries with others include: 1) making commitments or having sex when we really do not want to; 2) allowing people to say or do things that make us feel uncomfortable; and 3) feeling unable to deny inflammatory foods or behaviors that we know weaken us on some level.

Doing any combination of these things sends a message to the body that screams, "There are no boundaries in effect here! We are not safe! We need to launch an attack!"

The body's physical reaction to weak or overstepped boundaries is to release inflammatory agents that cause heat, redness, swelling, and adhesions; all of which represent the body's intention to safeguard the area. Unfortunately, this engenders an internal battle that ultimately works against our fertility. "Auto-immune" infertility conditions begin as our immune system releases high levels of antibodies intended to fight foreign invaders, but instead attack our own body's cells, many of which play a role in sustaining pregnancy.

Understand that the uterus is not an impenetrable organ isolated from the rest of the body. As your second heart, it is affected by how you feel about what you permit to occur inside your physical and psychological space. Just as the uterus is our second heart, the vagina serves as our second *brain*. Previous sexual violations as well as low self-esteem together create an environment where the brain hears a message of danger, and the body has the responsibility to respond in some way.

When we feel safe, we subconsciously send a message down to our ovaries, our second heart, and our second brain via the nervous system. The message confirms that what we are saying to others is in truthful alignment with what we are thinking inside. The body hears: "It is safe to ovulate. It is safe to conceive. It is safe carry to full-term."

The opposite scenario also holds true and offers another explanation for "unexplained" infertility. We derive no benefit in putting our needs last, or taking on another person's negativity, stress, verbal or physical abuse, or anger. With only weak boundaries in place to defend our integrity, the uterus functions as a sponge, soaking in fear and perceived violations and absorbing toxic emotions from other people. If a woman is unable to speak up and take care of herself in these scenarios, the body will act accordingly by denying the ability to reproduce, especially if conditions are chronically perceived as too stressful.

Infertility is one powerful way the body asserts some form of self-protection; it is the body's way of saying, "No. It is not safe to be pregnant under these conditions. We are constantly under attack. We will not make ourselves more vulnerable by creating a child, thank you very much."

I consistently see certain reproductive pathologies in women who exercise poor boundaries or have a history of boundaries issues. Some examples of relevant medical conditions include: endometriosis, fibroids, eggs that are allergic to their partner's semen, cervical mucus that is "hostile" to sperm, sticky blood that suffocates dividing fetal cells, and maternal antibodies that kill fetal cells.

Quite often, women with these conditions are harboring some old resentments, or they are still saying yes to too many things when they should be saying no. When we talk through these issues, these women's lives change for the better, as the desire to be a mother is strong enough to help them surrender these toxic patterns.

Western medicine provides surgeries, medications, blood thinners and steroids to address the physical symptoms and lab values that present in these immune reactions. Those treatments are effective at eliminating or reducing the outward symptoms of disease, and there is definitely a need for such infertility treatment. But surgery and meds do little to address the emotional patterns typically lying at the root of these immune dysfunctions.

Almost inevitably, a lack of clear boundaries between an afflicted woman and the people in her life will lead to some physical ailment somewhere. When we honestly assess our lives and notice that our words, our actions, and our true desires are not matching up, we need to find the courage to speak up. Honoring our life, our values, and our priorities will ultimately get us to our best and most fertile self.

When to Say Yes or No in Life

Alice was a teacher's aide. Known as a very considerate and funny woman, she always took care of everyone's feelings. She came from a large family and had a huge community of friends. This inclination to "take care of everyone else" led Alice into a history of repeated sexual abuse by a family member that lasted several years when she was growing up. Although she reported these incidents to her close relatives, no action was ever taken by the family to expose this awful truth. She was left feeling confused, guilty, and seething with repressed anger.

When Alice started acupuncture, she had taken on numerous extra commitments, over-obligating herself so much that she easily started crying in the office at each appointment. She said she knew she should make a change in her family dynamic by setting some boundaries. But she was nervous about upsetting everyone by initiating new behavior.

Determined to get to her baby, Alice persisted. She stopped spreading herself thin with family phone calls, visits, updates about her upcoming IVF cycle, and collecting everyone's opinion or advice. Instead, she made a firm announcement to everyone that she was completely "off limits." Furthermore, she would be saying "no" to absolutely anything that did not benefit her until the cycle was over.

During this quiet time, Alice worked with me, moving through a lot of the shame and painful memories associated with her abuse history. We worked together to reconcile her grief and process the resentment she had. As a result of setting the boundaries to create this free time for introspection, she came to the conclusion that her heart did not have enough room for the guilt and old resentments, and love for a child.

She also realized that the simple act of firmly saying "no" to various commitments gave her the space and time she needed to focus on ways to be her best self. With this, Alice vowed to practice better boundaries with everyone, even after her IVF cycle. She took the idea of boundaries work very seriously and continued the work even after she conceived.

Alice eventually learned to release the pain and shame of her past; and she forgave herself, as well as her male relative. During her pregnancy she developed a clear understanding of her boundaries, and felt safe knowing he would never be allowed to cross those boundaries again.

Alice was able to heal and grow so far, so fast in large part because of her willingness to embrace the present moment. She took responsibility for the ways in which she had allowed herself to remain stuck in her old trauma. As a result, she completely changed her family dynamic, insisting that her needs for space and respect be honored if the family wanted to be a part of her daughter's life. Each firmly set boundary strengthened her and helped her heal. Her family actually grew closer as a result of her courage.

When her daughter was about one-year-old, she returned to our office for help conceiving a second child. At this time, her new family dynamic was great, much healthier than it had been in years. Her husband's business was really taking off and making substantial profit—enough to afford a new house and provide them the opportunity to go straight to IVF if their first IUI attempt failed.

There was so much good stuff happening for them that she was having anxiety. She admitted feeling undeserving of so much happiness.

In preparing her for this second round of treatments, with good boundaries clearly intact, we focused on the popular and ever-powerful "Law of Attraction." This universal spiritual law says we attract precisely what we think about. If Alice chose to focus on how unworthy she was, she would push abundance away. She set a new boundary to protect herself from her own old, limited beliefs, and incorporated these simple words: "I deserve all this, and better!" and "I am open and ready to receive." We agreed that with these thought forms in place she would, without doubt, bring another child into the world, because the universal energy follows our thoughts.

The Law of Attraction says the universe contains an endless supply of abundance, and continuously gives us what we think we deserve — not what we want, because "to want" implies that we don't have something. Focusing continuously on how much we *want* something only creates more want for it. Once Alice grasped this tricky spiritual concept, she found herself saying, "Yes!" to everything presented to her, but not in a way that violated her boundaries. She let "abundance" become a new and important part of her vocabulary. Previously, she had to say no and insist on healthy limits. In this second IVF cycle, she was being asked to let down her guard, trust that she was safe and deserving, then say yes. She gave herself permission to receive everything good!

Both embryos transferred during that IVF cycle implanted successfully and grew into a healthy boy and girl. Alice went forward in abundance, growing twins while focusing constantly on the happy things she had created in her life by showing up for herself consistently.

Chapter 18

Awaken Your Creative Potential

Women today have become successful in their careers by relying on their intellect and solving multi-faceted problems. The majority of these intelligent and savvy women will approach infertility strategically, seeing it as a goal to achieve or a crisis they can manage. They often think that sex, conception, and/or IVF can be intellectualized, optimized, and scheduled into their cell phone calendars. When baby eludes them, these women employ even more of their brains; overanalyzing every aspect of the process, convinced that baby-making is a problem they can figure out in their heads.

Without meaning to, a woman can let her brain become her biggest obstacle to getting pregnant.

To offset this reliance on problem solving, we remind women of their inherent ability to *create*. We explain that a woman's need to create is equivalent to a man's need to provide; it is instinctual. Our creative ability is an inseparable component of who we are as women. Whether we are making a baby, writing a book, or tending a garden... if we are bringing things to life - we will feel fully alive!

What a mixed message we send to our wombs, the organ designed specifically for *creating children,* when we downplay our inherent female creativity and instead tell ourselves that creating a baby is about properly timed relations, good gametes, optimal lab values, and/or working with the right doctor.

I have seen previously artistic fertility patients begin to limit or halt their creative pursuits in order to concentrate on getting pregnant. Ironically, over-intellectualizing and stressing about our hormone interactions and gametes' natural functioning is the precise environment that leads ovaries to form cysts. The stress leads to hormonal imbalance, which often inhibits ovulation and cancels IVF cycles. How frustrating that is for women who refer to themselves as "planners."

Consider that the ovaries contain our seeds of creative potential. Blocking our creativity will energetically block the free flow of ovulation and hinder its proper timing. If we become too heady and deny our creative flow, should we really expect to easily create a child?

Most infertile patients would rather read infertility books and purchase fertility supplements than pick up a paintbrush or writing journal to express themselves for a few hours. This observation demonstrates how we are lessening our creative expression in exchange for an intellectual experience.

We would want our daughters to access their creativity and make things that touch and inspire others. Yet, we're quick to abandon that part of ourselves when we want to get pregnant. Is it possible to access your creative inner child and allow her to have fun gardening, painting, learning to knit a scarf, or trying a completely new style of cooking? Remember, pregnancy is the ultimate creative process. Getting reacquainted with latent creative talents would likely increase your fertility!

Each day, or as often as possible, women facing infertility need to set the intention to *create something, no matter how small or seemingly insignificant.* They must discover or unblock their creativity, embrace it fully, and begin merging creative energy into the science of conception.

IVF patients are given multiple prescriptions for various hormone injection mixtures and keep almost daily appointments. The stage is set for them to over-intellectualize the process. I imagine many women probably feel like scientists conducting experiments in their bathrooms with all those tiny vials and needles; they must prepare their hormone injections, remember to change their estrogen patches, insert suppositories, and set timer alerts on their phones to administer the right shots at the right time. The process requires they be precise, methodical, and reliant on their intellect.

Blending creativity into this meticulous science restores a sense of feminine balance and allows women to access both science and spirit, thus raising the chance of making a healthy baby and redirecting the course of their lives.

Being creative is an inherent part of being a woman. When we allow the science to overtake our creativity, we shortchange ourselves in a process that is all about creating. Instead, we can make a conscious effort to stay in the inspired mindset of creative possibility, while performing the due diligence necessary of high tech science.

Remember, we are not only creating a baby in this process, we are creating the environment that will allow us to redirect the flow of our lives in an entirely new direction.

Suppose it takes two years — or more — to facilitate a successful pregnancy. What memories do you want to have when you look back on the course of those years? Do you want to look back on two years of a punishing roller coaster ride of treatments? Or do you want to look back at that time as a journey into self-discovery and greater wisdom?

Life can stick it to us by increasing daily pressures and putting more demands on our time. Scheduling fertility treatments gives women an excuse to give up the creative, more "time-consuming" things they enjoy that might actually help them relax and strengthen their reproductive ability. They do not consider that they could be hurting their chances of conceiving by letting these things fall by the wayside.

Maybe you're an excellent cook, or a fabulous decorator. Or perhaps you have an unrealized knack for designing greeting cards or jewelry.

Maybe you love to paint watercolors or sketch, create vision boards or photo books.

What unfinished creative projects are you avoiding that may be calling out for your attention and might actually be *fun*? How inspiring and symbolic it is for creative projects to reach completion... especially for a woman struggling with infertility.

Consider that your ability to create a life is tied to your ability to create in general. As you begin increasing the amount of time you spend on creative outlets in your life, watch closely as your body responds with increased fertility. The signs may be small at first. Perhaps increased cervical mucus will appear at ovulation, or that confusing symptom of irregular spotting will "go away." Maybe your tendency to form ovarian cysts will stop and your menstrual cycle will regulate itself. Or you may notice your cramps have significantly lessened. All of these are signs of a lusciously creative and more fertile woman.

Creating the Well Women Acupuncture Office

When I learned my fallopian tube was blocked I started looking for ways to restore the overall flow of energy in my life. Since I spent so many hours working, I began this journey by redesigning our office space. Using a Feng Shui book for guidance, I set the intention to find and remove, or change, whatever was causing obstruction, and employed remedies to restore the free flow of energy.

I sketched new floor plans, created a comfortable interior layout and soon manifested the help of a carpenter friend. I asked Anna to help me select a warm, feminine color scheme. She then contributed paintings, wall hangings, and other artsy, handmade creations. Our receptionist shared her creative talent, infusing the office with sensual aromas, relaxed lighting, and a light sense of humor to soothe the spirits of tense patients when they arrived for their appointments.

Over the years, I created collages (also known as "vision boards") to represent where I was in my healing journey. Each board reveals a spiritual healing theme and has the ability to remind patients of certain transformative messages they could apply to their own lives. One collage emphasizes the importance of staying open. Another reflects on the power of love and sexual healing. A third signifies possibilities, and yet one more suggests fully accepting our lives.

These collages reveal clearly the physical and/or emotional state I was in when I put each one together. How powerful and healing it was for me to collect magazine clippings and paste them on a big board, declaring what was important to me at the time and reflecting what I saw as "possible" for my life.

I pasted pictures of healthy female bodies, including belly dancers, yoga students, and pregnant women. Then I added several empowering healing phrases to remind myself it was feasible to recover my fertility. I featured words and phrases like: "Courage," "Willing," "Peaceful mind, healthy body," "The Power of Love," "Empowered," etc. These handmade creative works of art previously resided in my apartment, and now hang on the walls in the office. They provide suggestions to other women of something creative they might like to do.

The blend of our individual talents and combined healing intention created a space that makes women feel as if they have entered a calm, nurturing womb. This feeling helps them relax instantly once they enter the office.

Before effortlessly having two children of her own, Anna used to design jewelry to offer for sale at the office. Each unique piece was created with a healing intention and was made with crystals and stones used specifically to balance women's disorders and female issues. Many women purchased and wore these pieces as they tried to conceive. Once they became pregnant, the women continued wearing their stones until their healthy baby arrived.

It was mind-blowing to watch Anna's creative goodies help heal so many women's troubled spirits. I think the pieces allowed the women to have something beautiful reminding them frequently that, indeed, they were doing something to heal their bodies. Of course, I purchased several pieces for myself!

As intended, my fallopian tube responded to my repeating the words "open" and "restored free flow." These were the messages on my vision boards. However, the improved flow in my body's energy was not only from the artwork, new floor plan, jewelry, and color scheme.

I realized that each acupuncture treatment I give my patients requires me to activate my creativity to keep the treatments fresh, personalized, and rich with healing potential. The ability to quickly deliver what each woman needs before she lies down to receive needles insists that I must have tremendous creativity! Owning that I had cultivated such a plentitude of creative energy helped me redirect my mind, spirit, tubes, and the rest of my reproductive tract towards healing. As a result, I became open to *even more* possibility.

Chapter 19

Say Goodbye to Pain

The word "goodbye" reeks of finality. However, this one word (when reframed and understood differently) holds the key to emotional resolution, and can be pivotal in helping us move forward.

When I entered acupuncture school, I began working with Debi Frankle, a marriage and family therapist who specializes in grief recovery in Calabasas, California. Feeling confused at first, I resisted her emphasis on grief recovery in my case, because I did not think I was grieving anything. I was seeking counseling to reconcile events in my past and I wanted to feel psychologically healthy enough to help my future patients do the same. But honestly, did I need *Grief Recovery*? No one had died. What exactly was I *grieving*? And why did she continuously present grief recovery as my salvation?

Later I came to understand that universal forces had not made a mistake; I was exactly where I was supposed to be. I worked with Debi during the four years of acupuncture school. She instilled in me the true healing potential of grieving *properly*. I learned that knowing how to use the correct emotional tools makes it is possible to live happily in the present moment. Painful experiences can be rerouted to a place in the brain known as The Past. From that space, memories could no longer override or prevent my current joys.

Debi guided me through *The Grief Recovery Handbook*, by John James and Russell Friedman. We worked together on the exercises laid out in the book; recounting my past experiences in order to identify the "losses" I was grieving (lost childhood, lost loves, lost innocence, loss of self-esteem, and lost health were just a few losses along my path). She taught me how to reframe my perspective about loss, and that helped me reduce the tragic impact those events continued to have on my present life.

To summarize, the handbook postulates that, as a society, we have been taught to fear the grieving process and we are ill prepared to deal with loss in general. Grief is a *normal and natural response to loss*, with loss being defined as a *change* from a familiar way of being. Grief is further defined as a conflicting *set of different emotions*, which makes it hard to reconcile intellectually. When a person is grieving, there are usually several different emotions/feelings happening simultaneously.

Our current bereavement trend is to find different ways to lessen the pain in our hearts. We pick up subconscious messages instructing us to cry alone and not for too long, lest we make other people uncomfortable with our heavy emotions. We are told to keep busy and let time heal us. However, it is not the amount of time passed that heals, but *what we do with the time* that will make the difference and lead to true resolution.

I have found the methods presented in *The Grief Recovery Handbook* to be outstandingly effective in reconstructing the hearts of infertile women. The book is a quick and easy read that offers a handful of empowering exercises designed to first expose the individual's unique losses, then help readers say goodbye *to the pain* caused by loss.

The hundreds of women to whom I have recommended the book used it to empower themselves, integrating its simple approach. Though it is a generalized grief book not focused on fertility, women who have suffered miscarriages, stillbirths, or repeated disappointment benefit from it tremendously.

In the case of infertility, grief resolution can be that one thing that facilitates a necessary "A-ha!" moment and yields the emotional shift that finally allows conception and successful pregnancy. Given the high number of women I have treated successfully using the ideas laid out in *The Grief*

Recovery Handbook, I've concluded that the coping skills we've learned in our society provide us with very little sense of resolve.

With respect to infertility and its myriad losses, consider that holding on to emotional pain and disappointment keeps us stuck emotionally. We get trapped mentally processing *what has happened* and *what might never happen*. Without proper grieving tools, we can find ourselves literally paralyzed in our heads, clinging to painful experiences from the past while worrying endlessly about the future. This behavior causes people to shut down and isolate, or reflexively overreact to situations that happen if their lives, as if the original trauma is happening all over again.

Resolving grief creates the necessary open space in our minds and in our hearts, leaving room for new loves, new babies, and happier experiences. Proper grief recovery isn't so much the act of saying goodbye to a lost loved one. It is more about the act of releasing the pain and resentment caused by their departure. We have a responsibility to ourselves to release painful thoughts and say, "For my own well-being and highest good of everyone involved, I'm ready to move on from this pain."

When I am working with a grieving patient, I encourage her to take a moment to fully feel a painful memory; because releasing a few tears will help her access more space within her heart. While no one enjoys crying or feeling vulnerable in front of others, it feels good to release some emotional pain. In Chinese medicine, tears are known as the "fluid of the heart." Therefore, we should not fear tears. They have enormous healing potential.

Do not let another day go by holding tears inside, thinking you need to "stay strong" or "just let it go."

Instead, write powerful letters to the children who have left your life due to miscarriage, abortion, still-birth, nonviable pregnancies, or otherwise. Consider holding some type of memorial service to acknowledge and honor the children who lived in your womb, no matter how briefly.

Grieving any significant lost loves and saying goodbye to the pain of unfinished or heartbreaking relationships (babies and otherwise) will work wonders to heal old wounds and create open space, giving you the opportunity to say hello to something new.

Finding the Strength to Say Goodbye

Alisa faced one of the most challenging situations I have ever witnessed. As a result, she is without a doubt one of the most inspirational women I have worked with.

At age thirty-two, Lisa conceived twins via IVF. She was originally diagnosed with polycystic ovaries and suffered a miscarriage two years prior. This second pregnancy had progressed normally until week nineteen, when she developed an incompetent cervix following her earlier CVS testing. The treatment of her cervix required a stitching procedure, from which she unknowingly contracted a bacterial infection.

For weeks she had no symptoms, therefore had no idea her babies were in danger. Suddenly, at week twenty-three, Alisa developed a fever and went into spontaneous labor. The twins were not viable at that early stage of pregnancy, and their lives ended within minutes of being outside the womb. Alisa was not able to look at them in the ER for the short time they were alive. She feared that she would literally explode from the emotional intensity and heartache.

It took several months to heal her traumatized body before she could even begin to address her emotions. When she thought she might be ready to start IVF again using her frozen embryos, she came back to our office. We sat together while she cried, mourning the two children. It was one of few times I found myself at a loss for words.

Alisa soldiered on, but one IVF attempt after another with her remaining thirty frozen embryos resulted in no pregnancies.

There were two things happening that prevented another pregnancy. On the physical level, her doctor reviewed prior HSG films and discovered that she had a uterine septum, which hindered proper thickening of the endometrium and was preventing implantation. On a psycho-spiritual level, Alisa was creating a barrier as well. She was not able to get beyond the fear of carrying multiples again, nor could she get past the thought of losing another baby.

As she sat with me discussing these fertility obstacles, Alisa had so much unresolved grief that she could not stop crying.

Each week in our office, I volunteered to partner up with her to do some grief recovery work. She would get started, then soon need to pull back. I waited patiently until she was clearly ready to do the exercises laid out in the book. Finally, we got to the "Goodbye Letter."

Her emotional release was incomparable. The tears, pain, and raw emotions that came out of her must have weighed ten pounds, because she looked that much lighter when she left. Listening intently, I could not hold back my own tears. It was riveting to watch someone use words and feelings to release attachment and pain from such insurmountable loss.

I now know women can transform *anything*, thanks to the courage this young woman demonstrated in our office that day.

In the weeks that followed, Alisa repeatedly said she felt increasingly better. She confided that even nearly one year later, she still had not been able to open the door to what would have been the twins' room. Behind that door sat paint cans, unopened boxes that housed their cribs, and several bags of clothes, blankets and stuffed toys.

We constructed a plan to help her honor her children. Soon after, she declared that she finally had the courage to open the door, empty the room, cry if she felt like it, and paint the walls a new color. We also agreed she would pick a day on the calendar to hold a service with her husband and read her goodbye letter out loud to him. The service was intended to acknowledge that the two *had lived*, but were no longer here. I had no idea if she (or anyone) could muster that much courage, but as I have said, the women I have the privilege of working with are nothing short of amazing.

When she came back to the office a few weeks later, she had accomplished everything! There was such obvious lightness in her heart. Those babies were set free, and she was too. She said she felt like their spirits had been released from that room, and said she was much happier inside, having been able to honor them in this memorable way.

She conceived with her next frozen embryo transfer, and although the pregnancy required complete bed rest from the beginning to maintain a secure cervix, she allowed the time to be about resting and healing. Nine months later, Alisa delivered a full-term, healthy baby girl.

Chapter 20

Identify the Tiger in Your Life

With respect to evolution, our response to stress does not appear to have advanced far beyond our more primitive ancestors. Yet, we must still find ways to accommodate the more chronic forms of stress we experience today. Our modern nervous systems cannot differentiate whether we are being chased by a tiger or working fourteen-hour days to afford our expensive lifestyles. The body perceives both forms of stress as a threat to survival.

A human being running from a vicious tiger needs to function at a maximum performance level. The body will rely on the strength and efficiency of the nervous system to secrete adrenaline and cortisol, and will speed up the cardiovascular and pulmonary systems. In response to high levels of stress, the body will shut down the other systems not involved in the escape. Digestion will halt temporarily and ovaries will delay ovulation.

This biological hardwiring obviously hinders a woman's ability to get pregnant. Stress that is chronic can make conception nearly impossible from this physiological standpoint. The body's logic is that pregnancy and caring for young makes someone too vulnerable during times of threatened survival. Therefore, a body experiencing chronic stress will respond to the stress by negatively impacting the reproductive system.

What a brilliant design for humans who are outrunning wild animals. But it's not so great for women who have succeeded in life relying on the energizing effects of adrenaline, who now want to create a baby.

Without realizing it, these "Type A" women have done considerable (and sometimes irreversible) damage to their reproductive systems.

Their nervous system's communication with other systems probably goes something like, "Alert! Our survival is threatened. Shut down the ovaries. Clench the fallopian tubes. Create barriers for the sperm. If we get pregnant we will be too vulnerable to escape danger!"

If this seems silly, ask any pregnant woman to lace up their running shoes and sprint to the end of the street. Despite having abundant hormones, pregnant women are highly vulnerable creatures in terms of being able to get anywhere fast. From a survival standpoint, pregnancy represents the least desirable condition for a body in times of stress.

Money worries, sleepless nights, skipped meals, and a reliance on stimulating caffeine and sugar will all contribute to the release of excess stress hormones in a woman's bloodstream and suggest her likeliness to have reproductive trouble.

Instead of basking in an estrogen-rich environment, with abundant endorphins and serotonin, all of which relax the nervous system, the developing follicles of highly stressed women are constantly exposed to a toxic burden of stress hormones adrenaline and cortisol.

As a result, certain conditions such as elevated FSH, hypothalamic ovulatory dysfunction, early menopause symptoms, and erratic menstrual cycles are typically found in these women. Deprived of healthy levels of estrogen on a consistent basis, these women's follicles may not mature properly to yield good quality eggs, or anovulatory cycles may result, preventing conception month after month (even if cycle lengths appear to be the same).

Modalities such as acupuncture, biofeedback, hypnosis, mind-body techniques, and spiritual practices like meditation all help to reverse the situation by releasing endorphins and serotonin into the bloodstream. Each of these therapies impacts the brain and nervous system in a positive way, yielding deeper feelings of peace and well-being.

I have needled some of the most tightly wound, stressed out women who come to the office after work, after sitting in traffic, or after getting more bad news from their MDs about their fertility. These harried women arrive late to their appointments with frantic explanations, dilated pupils, tight necks and shoulders, shortness of breath, full bladders and empty stomachs. They do not realize how stressed they are because they have become used to this lifestyle. However, their outward appearances mimic those of people in danger.

What can we do about this? My staff and I focus on educating women who appear to be in this situation. We figure that, until now, they haven't known that their behavior impacts their fertility.

In the most gentle ways possible, we alert them to the following harsh realities: 1) They are not machines who can just power through without consequence; 2) Unlike men, women do not have daily renewed stores of testosterone to finance their stressful lives, and therefore are more predisposed to adrenal exhaustion as they rely on adrenaline to reach deadlines; 3) In the presence of constant exposure to adrenaline and cortisol, chronically stressed women are harming their ovaries; 4) They need to make the conscious decision to cut stress down wherever possible (by working fewer hours, delegating responsibilities, turning off phones and computers by 8 pm, etc.); and 5) They need to begin restoring their female health by increasing exposure to endorphins and oxytocin. We suggest incorporating acupuncture, massage, hypnotherapy, meditation, and more relaxed times with loved ones, particularly female friends.

Feelings of despair are caused by stressful thoughts, such as, "I've got so much to do. I'll never get all this done. How am I going to accomplish everything?" The woman who is ready to heal infertility tells herself, "I am at peace. I trust that whatever needs to be done, will get done. I can do better work when I am relaxed and rested. There is peace all around me. This is just a deadline; my survival is not threatened."

Our bodies are very powerful and can do a lot with very little. Relaxing your body and supplying it with restorative, reassuring, peaceful thoughts will go a long way to reverse the damage caused by stress.

Imagine an ON/OFF switch inside your brain. Your new, relaxed attitude about stress has the ability to flip infertility OFF, while flipping fertility back into the ON position. Find as many times during your day as possible that you can allow your mind to feel this calm, peaceful way of being. Become practiced at looking differently at your life and allow yourself to hear any message your personal stress may be trying to tell you.

Turning Fertility ON after an FSH score of 79!

Unemployed actress and full-time student, Tina arrived at Well Women when she was almost forty-years-old. On a level of one to ten, she reported that her stress felt like a nine. Stress came from school deadlines, numerous auditions that led nowhere, and the financial worries of living between jobs, as her husband also worked in the entertainment industry as a writer.

Her estradiol score was low as a result of being in this state of "constant unrest," as she described it. Her cycles were short (sixteen to twenty-two days) and it had been ages since she'd seen any cervical mucus. She reported a lowered libido and disrupted sleep that was often filled with vivid dreams. She disclosed at the first appointment that she was adopted and had always felt incomplete, like a puzzle with one missing piece. This feeling likely motivated her to try with such tenacity to make it as an actress and have a successful career.

I suggested she begin adding more red meat to her diet in order to feel more grounded, as her physique was rather frail, thin, and wiry (much like a model), and her demeanor was rather nervous. We also agreed that she would benefit from adding whole-fat, unpasteurized dairy products.

This is the one woman whom I actually encouraged to eat ice cream, thinking the young girl inside who felt abandoned might feel nurtured having such a treat; meanwhile, the woman she had become needed the fat to slow down her ovarian function and restore a more normal cycle length. I wasn't worried about the sugar content of the ice cream, because I believed she desperately needed dairy fat to calm her nerves.

When she returned several weeks later, she said she had implemented all the dietary suggestions and was surprised by what a difference it had made. She even had cervical fluid again!

As we worked together, I explained how her body perceived the threat of a "looming tiger" based on her chronic stress and her attitude about it. The next month she checked her FSH levels for the first time and was shocked to hear her score was 23. The doctor told her she had diminished ovarian reserve. He wanted her to take birth control pills and return the following month. If her score was lowered, he said they would stimulate her ovaries and do insemination.

This plan further stressed her out, due to finances and the thought of taking various hormones when she was all about doing things naturally.

Knowing adrenal stress depletes the body of essential minerals such as magnesium, potassium, and calcium, I suggested she consume mineral-rich leafy greens every day and add Maca root powder to her cereal and yogurt because of its high level of B vitamins, another nutrient of which the body is robbed in times of high stress.

That month, they moved to a new apartment and her stress level increased. Not just because of the stress of moving, but because she now had the stress of being told she was a patient with infertility. This stress affected her greatly and her sleep pattern became even more erratic. Her next FSH score was 79.

She admitted she had not taken my advice about the greens and Maca powder because she was too stressed. However, to see her score jump so dramatically in such a short period of time elevated her stress to a near panic. She explained that because she was adopted, donor eggs would not ever be an option for her. On a very innate, primal level, she needed to know there was someone she could love who shared her genes.

Tina sought a second and third opinion. One doctor actually laughed at her when she explained that she was planning to use acupuncture and diet to help bring her FSH score down.

If she was not in the market for donor eggs and the doctors were convinced that she would not conceive given her high FSH scores, she was left with no choice but to put all of her faith into her acupuncture treatments and lifestyle changes. So, we decided to step it up.

She began getting treatments three times a week. I adjusted the cost of treatment to almost nothing, feeling such a connection to this woman who had a story somewhat similar to my own. I believed that if she could tip the scale in favor of more endorphins in her system than adrenaline, she could probably have a baby, so I became her ally and we decided to face this challenge together. We also agreed on no more testing of FSH, inclusion of mineral rich greens every day without fail, Maca powder, meditation, one less class at school, more time spent doing art that she enjoyed, and, at the root of everything, a spiritual understanding that these acts of nurturing herself were very important for her overall healing. Perhaps this strategy held the power to lead her to that "one missing puzzle piece."

It took seven months of such frequent treatments to optimize her body, reset her nervous system, and restore her tired spirit, but she and her husband conceived a healthy baby girl naturally and proved that the body really is capable of refreshing itself when there is less of a perceived threat to survival.

Chapter 21

Conquer Fear with Wisdom

According to Chinese medicine, fear is the emotion that corresponds with the kidney system, and our kidney "essence" dictates our reproductive ability. Therefore, fertility-focused acupuncturists can be very effective with treatment when they help patients unravel and move beyond their deepest, hidden fears.

Kidney essence is inherited from our parents. It's our genetic blueprinting, determined for us at the time of conception, and it's what we use to finance our reproductive efforts. Much like an investment savings account, the kidney essence is reserved for making the "big purchases" in life, such as procreating.

Being fearful or afraid depletes the kidneys and indirectly hinders our fertility as a result. Looming fears and chronic anxiety constitute large withdrawals from the kidney essence, and therefore, have a negative impact on our ability to get pregnant.

Uncertainty is at the root of the fears and anxiety that surround infertile women. There is so much at stake, and no guarantee their vast efforts will lead to a healthy baby in the end. Fertility treatments are expensive; they interfere with a woman's normal hormone production and greatly affect her schedule and lifestyle. Her world becomes centered on an uncertain outcome, and that is nerve-wracking, for sure.

Ancient Chinese wisdom advises us to "conquer fear with wisdom." This suggests that we remember when or how we survived other frightening times in life, and focus on the wisdom that was gained from those experiences.

The personal strength, tests of character, and wisdom acquired from getting through nightmarish times are important resources to lean on while moving through this period of baby-making uncertainty. Rewind your life story and remember when you were nervous about getting married or attracting the right partner. Remember those times you experienced setbacks at work that left you feeling nervous about your ability to move forward in your chosen career. Those kinds of experiences have spiritual lessons embedded within them. When we survive life's toughest challenges, we gain necessary wisdom for our futures.

The emotions of fear and worry may, at first glance, seem similar, but they keep us paralyzed in different ways. Like a cat chasing its tail, worry is a circular thought pattern that leads nowhere, while fear grips a person with a sinking dreadfulness. Fear delivers a more "the floor is about to drop from underneath me" sensation.

In order to conquer fear with wisdom, you must consciously revisit previous times you felt this type of dread. Remember how you kept yourself safe, and employ that same logic now in order to empower yourself and calm the angst that uncertainty creates.

When my patients get blood work done or have certain diagnostic procedures, they may panic with the results. I explain to these patients that the findings need to be viewed objectively, rather than emotionally. I offer the idea that their bodies are communicating this information to their doctors, to allow the doctors to become better informed about their fertility so they can improve the women's odds of conceiving.

Those who can continuously find courage and keep fear in check end up becoming mothers. Either they will finally get pregnant naturally, choose adoption, or use donor eggs. These women use their hard-won wisdom to get ahead of their fears, realizing it's harmful to live in a state of constant panic. They make a conscious commitment to live in a place of peace and acceptance. They find ways to sit with the uncomfortable anxiety of not knowing whether procedures or acupuncture and diet/lifestyle changes will be successful. They feel more secure in themselves, regardless of the outcome.

For women who can conquer fear with wisdom, the fourteen days following ovulation pass a little more quickly and a lot less traumatically.

Sometimes we need to talk ourselves out of fear and anxiety using the comfort of a "Plan B." In the event that all attempts to have our own child fail to work, determined and fearless women can say to themselves, "I am intended to mother a child and I have enough love in my heart to raise one, even if he or she doesn't look like me. I have the courage to open my heart fully to adopting or other parenting options."

Wisdom comes from facing the challenges in life that provide us with opportunities to be our best selves. Ask yourself what fears you are running from. In what ways would your life change if you chose to conquer fear with wisdom?

Facing Fear, Once and for All

Mindy was a powerful career woman whose unresolved fears actually transformed into full-blown panic attacks during her attempts to conceive. This successful woman had a case of endometriosis and a gut-wrenching fear of being a complete failure in life. The deeply rooted fear of letting people down or being less than perfect was diminishing her reproductive essence.

She admitted that her life had very much been about proving herself, especially to her father. Although she had succeeded in the professional world, her inability to get pregnant was challenging her. It triggered a wild fear of inadequacy and made her literally panic that she would disappoint everyone in her life.

In an attempt to control her endometriosis before implanting embryos during IVF, her MD prescribed three months of continuous Lupron to suppress her cycles, following laparoscopic surgery to remove endometrial adhesions. The word "suppression" and his suggestion of a three-month recovery time was enough to bring on a major panic attack.

Three months. The thought of three more long months of facing continual fear of failing made her heart sink and left a racing feeling in her chest. She felt completely out of control.

I referred Mindy immediately to a psychotherapist who specializes in infertility, and the three of us began working as a team to help her feel safe enough to address these deeply rooted fears. I suggested that she reframe the three-month prescription of Lupron as an *excellent idea.* Those three months would give her time to acknowledge the source of her fears, as well as the opportunity to thoroughly address her discoveries in therapy. She agreed!

One day during acupuncture, I explained how it appeared that she was "plugging" her thoughts and energy into a fear-based belief that she was failing somehow. In reality, she was anything but a failure. In the course of our conversation, we uncovered Mindy's deeply hidden belief that, if she failed, her father would no longer love her. We recognized that, to her subconscious mind, the loss of her father's affection equaled the loss of his protection. Therefore, this potential loss posed a threat to her survival. It was a very instinctual feeling, and it mimicked free-falling; possibly to her death. The feeling triggered her to hyperventilate and feel afraid, like she was going to die.

As we talked, as Mindy heard herself say these things aloud, she realized her fears were unfounded. She would never have been kicked out of her home with nowhere to go. She would never have lost her father's love. With greater understanding, she realized that she'd "plugged in" to these fear-based insecurities. Mindy began to see that she could "unplug" her energy from all of those perceived negative consequences she had subconsciously conjured up whenever she wanted. She could forever use this new wisdom to calm those looming fears.

During acupuncture, under the influence of endorphins, Mindy felt safe. She also felt safe in therapy, where she vocalized all her fears and saw that the world didn't come to an end! Her life didn't fall apart when she admitted she was afraid. She learned that fears are just low vibration energy patterns. She could choose whether to plug into them and give them her energy, or not.

Soon the idea of "unplugging" and using inner wisdom to conquer fear became her more practiced way of being. Week after week during those three months, she appeared for acupuncture and continued her therapy sessions. Her panic attacks became fewer and lessened in duration and intensity. The attacks that previously occurred every time she got into her car became reduced to once per week, and eventually did not come back.

At the end of the three months of Lupron, Mindy proceeded with her next IVF. It was no surprise that, after all that effort, this was the time she conceived her son. Mindy continued acupuncture through her entire pregnancy and enjoyed the calm time to connect with the baby.

One of my biggest professional compliments came the day her husband came in to pick up a refill of her herbs long before she conceived. He sincerely thanked me for the work I had done with his wife. The changes Mindy had made from our conversations and the acupuncture sessions made a profoundly positive impact on their marriage.

"I don't know what goes on during these sessions," he said, "but it works! Thank you for getting my wife back."

Chapter 22

Reframe Disappointment

Specific to infertility is the challenging issue of facing heart-wrenching disappointment every single month. Every time we have to "face the stick," whether it's to detect surging LH at ovulation or to confirm early pregnancy, we must deal with the harsh likelihood of being disappointed yet again.

For women having a hard time resolving infertility, a blank stick represents another failure. It's another reason to feel worthless, broken, or not destined to be a mother. Feeling pessimistic is easy when you've been trying for months, or even years. Some of my patients have been attempting to get pregnant for more than a decade without success. That's a lot of times to be disappointed and a lot of losses to overcome—lost time, lost dreams, lost faith, lost hope. Only a psychologically healthy and spiritually "well" woman could manage to enjoy her life fully, having been stuck that many times with disappointment.

All that said, facing disappointment time and again can possibly force us into increased self-awareness and help us find other routes to fulfillment, peace, or joy. Repeated disappointment motivates some people to find prayer or meditation, hypnotherapy or acupuncture. These modalities are proven to help restore a sense of inner peace. Facing the disappointments inherent in infertility often leads women to find these activities that otherwise might never appeal to her.

The women and couples who thrive despite facing disappointment typically incorporate alternative forms of healing and psychotherapy to address the intense pressure. Doing so helps them develop more spiritual strength to offer their children (possibly adopted or otherwise conceived) when they finally do arrive. Or it prepares them to move on with their lives, feeling resolved about their attempts to become parents.

Maintaining self-respect and self-love while facing disappointment involves acknowledging that you consistently tried your best to reach a successful outcome. Facing disappointment also requires you to develop the necessary ability to detach somewhat from the baby-making pursuit. Much like waiting for the proverbial phone to ring while dating, things tend shift in the direction you want when you accept the uncertainty of the situation fully. By embracing the inherent disappointments that are bound to come along, you can return to living your life "in the meantime."

Transforming disappointment is about having faith, listening to a higher power and repeatedly finding the determination to keep going regardless of how your circumstances may appear. If we recognize this time as an amazing and deeply transformational spiritual journey, we can see that a disappointment is also an opportunity... for something greater than a baby.

I sit in front of patients all the time who are so sad and disappointed that they are ready to give up. Sometimes these women will revert to feeling passive and hopeless, saying in a deflated tone, "I hope it works this time." I am right there to remind them, much like a coach, "No, we don't *hope* it works this time. We remember that we have the power to *allow* it to work, and we can set the intention for things to change. Let's instead say, 'I already know disappointment, now I am ready to know a positive outcome.'"

Keep asking yourself where you can grow or how you can become stronger. Find some degree of appreciation that each disappointment holds a potentially valuable lesson for you.

Transforming Disappointment

I remember when Eliza came in for her regularly scheduled acupuncture appointment after another failed IVF attempt. Eliza was a positive person and usually had an optimistic attitude surrounding this baby-making journey. As a naturopath, she had even helped a few of her own patients get through the infertility process.

On that day, however, she announced that her chief complaint was *pessimism*. Her complaints usually were common to other women going through infertility treatments—hormone imbalance, weight gain, abdomen and breast swelling. But that afternoon she used her own experience as a physician to give me a clear direction of where to guide her in treatment. She needed a pep talk to get back on track.

After life sticks us with enough disappointments, it pretty much insists we become open to new attitudes and ideas for moving forward. For instance, after an agreed-upon number of attempted inseminations or several rounds of IVF, it may become necessary to accept the idea of donor eggs, adoption, or fostering a child.

Such was the case with Eliza. She was forty, and had spent two years and several thousands of dollars attempting IVF using her own eggs. Each time she produced at least a dozen eggs, but there was always some complication with fertilization, or she suffered from hyper-stimulation, or she developed an allergic response to the hormones. Each time she hoped, she believed, she prayed, she trusted; each time she was disappointed.

The continual disappointment started to affect her self-esteem and her otherwise healthy new marriage. This woman, who usually took pride in making everyone in the office laugh with her jokes, said she was on the verge of "not liking her life anymore if it meant not being a mother." Her sad words are so common.

"We selected a donor!" Eliza announced at her next appointment. I was relieved. Then she added, "This will have to be our last attempt, because we borrowed money from everyone to be able to do it. I have been disappointed so many times. If it doesn't work this time, what will I tell everyone?"

"Yes," I said. "You've faced almost two years of disappointment. However, the reason to feel hopeful is NOT because you'll use younger eggs. The other consideration is that your spirit has been transformed by all this disappointment! Having the experience of repeated disappointment and *not giving up* is what has allowed you to manifest this opportunity! Everyone has agreed to help you financially because your determination is inspiring. They love the way you have triumphed over the disappointments enough to take your dream of becoming a parent to the next level. They are proud of you *simply for not giving up!*"

Eliza conceived on the first round of donor eggs. Had she given in to disappointment, she never would have known the joy of having a son to raise and love.

Chapter 23
Choose The Middle Path

If we live a life defined only by its successes, we will find ourselves living at one extreme or the other. Either we make it to our desired goal, or we have failed miserably. This type of all-or-nothing focused existence, based solely on achievements, leaves little appreciation for the experiences in between and the insights gained along the way.

There is a metaphorical place often referred to as "the gray area." It exists between black and white. It is the area that lies in between "all" and "nothing," between endless suffering in life and being where we think we wish to be. The gray area is a place worth discovering in our time on earth, because it's a place of inner peace, acceptance, and faith. It is the only place I can imagine where the possibility of genuine happiness actually exists.

This concept so easily applies to the fertility journey. People will say there is no in-between. If you want to have a baby, you cannot be "a little bit pregnant." However, I have seen infertile women transform their pain and once again become ripe with hope, full of passion, and living a life they believe is full of abundance. They are just as coveted as a woman sporting a swollen belly, if not more, because they've found true happiness and meaning in their lives. These women don't see their lives in terms of being either wildly fecund or completely barren.

Women who allow a gray area in their lives demonstrate a flexible personality that allows room for options, alternatives, and possibilities in order to experience fulfillment. Life in the gray doesn't insist on the attainment of some ideal. Instead, adopting this philosophy means you believe your life is ideal already, and you embrace it exactly as it is.

Women who live in a world of extremes describe their lives as being either "great" or "terrible," and they are frequently disappointed. With respect to getting pregnant, they are happy only around ovulation, when the possibility of manifesting their dream is the highest. They base their happiness on *someday* being pregnant and do not really want to fully participate in the days in between now and when that time comes. They rely on time-filling distractions to "survive" the two weeks between ovulation and menstruation. They postpone vacations in case they start an IVF cycle, and they fret endlessly about what they will do if it does not work.

The Buddhist philosophy of walking the "Middle Path" represents a life of balance that flows with and appreciates the natural timing of things. When women apply this logic to their previous "all or nothing, black or white" perspective, they come to appreciate the intangible middle, that nice shade of gray known as "being happy with my life."

There is a sense of inner peace and confidence that accompanies living in the gray. It is the peacefulness that comes from knowing yourself, loving your life and being passionate about your relationships, your career, and/ or your life purpose.

It's Not All Black or White

One of the brightest, most passionate women I have ever met learned to fully embrace this gray area after recovering from a history of alcoholism. At age forty, Stephanie showed up in our office. She described herself as a legal secretary by day and acting student by night. She lit up the room with her vibration and high enthusiasm for life. She has a very dynamic presence and secure sense of self.

Stephanie had structural infertility. This means her body was created with only one ovary, one kidney, and a smaller-than-normal uterus. However, after sixteen years of sobriety and self-cultivation, she developed such a positive attitude and appreciation for life that her aura illuminated our entire office every time she walked in; no one would guess she was so reproductively challenged.

She attempted IVF four times. There were two pregnancies, each very brief. Her doctors were not sure what caused the miscarriages, but shortly after those experiences she decided to start adoption proceedings. Some women might see the failed cycles as personal failures and keep chasing after the goal. This woman recognized the financial, emotional, and physical strain she had endured, and the stress it put on herself and her marriage.

Instead of looking at her life as "not pregnant and therefore not happy," she created a gray area in her mind. Stephanie embraced the *possibility* of motherhood happening naturally via unprotected, enjoyable sex, while she and her husband waited for the arrival of their soon-to-be-adopted Mandarin daughter.

Once she created this possibility for herself, her lifelong dream of becoming a successful actress also felt more complete. Instead of focusing on the roles she did not get, she focused on the personal growth she acquired in the acting classes. She appreciated having a platform to play out dramas and perform various roles, but no longer needed to become a famous actress to attribute value to her life.

Stephanie accepted her life as it was being played out before her, one day at a time. She felt triumph over the addictive aspect of her personality, the part of her that needed exhilaration, accomplishments, and drama to define her as an exciting woman.

She felt like she had won an academy award for the "movie" in which she played herself—a secure woman in a happy marriage, expecting an adopted child, and preparing for the challenges inherent in that endeavor. She left behind the preconceived idea that achieving full-term pregnancy was the utmost example of success.

Stephanie committed to loving every moment of her life as an expectant mother. Her life in the gray actually started to involve lots of color—in the form of picking paint swatches for a nursery!

Living in the gray.

Walking the Middle Path.

Striving for peace, balance and contentment in the life you have.

These are all examples of ultimate accomplishment.

Do you have a tendency towards an "all or nothing" approach to fertility? There are actually several options available to you in the gray area. Are you willing to reside there, even just for today?

Try to see all the spaces in between your two perceived endpoints—pregnant and not pregnant. Stop insisting that outcomes are only successful when they look how you thought they would, or how it looks in the lives of the people to whom you compare yourself. Try instead to love your world of gray, and consider new ways you can add a little more color.

Chapter 24

Release Anger

For those grappling with infertility, anger has the power to transform otherwise rational women into fire-breathing dragons with its explosive heat and passion. While angry women appear to be full of energy, this emotional, reckless energy is *consumptive*. It does absolutely nothing to help fertility.

Your anger or frustrations can be completely justified, but hanging on to resentment or stuffing down unexpressed rage will keep you stuck in the same negative space. "Stuck" women find it nearly impossible to get pregnant, which creates further reason to be mad as hell.

According to basic laws of physics, *energy can neither be created nor destroyed*. It transforms itself into other forms of energy. "Angry" energy is no different. Once anger is present, it doesn't go away until we express it or consciously decide to stop being mad about whatever got us so fired up. Unexpressed anger turns inward and is stored as resentment. Bitter seeds of resentment become weeds that compete with the space in our heart intended for experiences of joy and love.

Our attempts to become mothers appear to be hopeless with each cycle that is called off due to cysts or dominant follicles. Yet, these conditions repeatedly manifest in women who are already angry. A vicious cycle results and makes conception and pregnancy very challenging.

If infertility justifiably makes us angry and frustrated, yet anger and frustration work against our chances of becoming mothers, what are we to do? What steps should we take to release anger and create the likeliness of a happy miracle occurring in our lives?

First, we have to learn, understand, and appreciate the role of the liver energy in the body—then we will know when we need to detoxify and discharge anger. As in Western medicine, the liver in Chinese medicine is responsible for proper hormone balance and the processing of toxic emotions (anger and frustration), along with their byproducts (resentment). The liver system accomplishes these tasks by regulating the proper flow of qi (energy) throughout the body.

A person with healthy, free-flowing liver qi who is put into a maddening situation can be counted on to respond appropriately—reacting somewhere in the middle of complacency and rage. She expresses her feelings in a way that discharges fire and emotional heat, then moves on with her life. A person with a toxic liver will either resort to acts of aggression (engaging in frequent arguments), passivity (stuffing down feelings of rage), or will engage in a more complex, passive-aggressive form of behavior.

Free-flowing liver qi is perceived as consistent movement forward in the direction of our desires and goals. Conversely, disappointments, setbacks and frustrations stagnate the liver's energy and require something on our part to move through the stagnation. I typically recommend to my patients that they write, cry, run, punch pillows, talk it out, scream, or participate in any form of expression that will release the energy from their body. Once angry energy is released, the flow is restored and open space is created. Either something positive can fill the newly opened space, or the woman can return to her more peaceful self.

How Anger Stands in Our Way of Baby

Helene had already been attempting to get pregnant for two-and-one-half-years by the time she found the Well Women office. She was referred to me by two of my patients who, coincidentally, happened to be sitting with her in the waiting room at her fertility doctor's office. The woman on her left recommended Helene try our office to improve her perspective, and the woman sitting on her right side just happened to have an extra Well Women business card in her purse! An uptight woman in general, angry Helene was so impressed that two random women would recommend Well Women Acupuncture so highly, she called the office that same day.

Helene had good reason to be mad. At age thirty-five, she had already been pregnant three times, and each time the babies miscarried due to abnormal genetics. The first loss occurred at twenty weeks, when she learned her baby had a deformed heart, one kidney, and a brain defect. The second child, conceived one year later, was terminated at sixteen weeks when early screening revealed the same genetic abnormalities had occurred. The third pregnancy happened four months later, but did not manifest a heartbeat at the six-week ultrasound.

At the time of her first acupuncture appointment, Helene had recently been hyper-stimulated and was forced to cancel her current cycle. She emphasized having a desperate NEED to be in control of this out-of-control situation. She expressed how furious she was—at God, the world, other pregnant women, and her body—for not being able to hold her own healthy baby in her arms.

Both of the women who referred Helene to the office called me to "warn" me she was coming! That revealed how much her anger preceded her. But it was understandable. It did seem like a "baby carrot" had been dangled before her so many times. Each pregnancy allowed her to fully attach to the dream of becoming a mom. Then, nearly halfway through, the dream was gone without any explanation.

Helene responded immediately to the Well Women tactics of providing extra talk time and a safe space to release all of her feelings. She let her guard down so much that, for the first time in those two-and-one-half-years, she was able to relax, unwind, and entertain the thought of healing.

Over the next few months, Helene decompressed. Her hyper-stimulated ovaries, agitated liver, and disturbed spirit all improved from releasing this pent-up angry energy. She started taking herbs, cut down on sugar, and eliminated Splenda and Nutra-Sweet (as both are possible neurotoxins). She continued to nourish and soothe her liver with beneficial greens like spinach and dandelion.

Finally, she was ready for her next IUI. She produced several follicles and felt optimistic. When the cycle did not result in pregnancy, she returned to agitation and irritability. But this time, she acknowledged that not only was she mad at God for taking these children, she was also blaming "him" for killing her mother with cancer three years prior. We again discussed how destructive it was for her to carry all that pathological energy around with her all the time.

We came up with possible ways she could release it, such as kickboxing, hitting punching bags at the gym, throwing stones into the ocean, and even screaming in the car—anything physical that was capable of getting that toxic energy and those negative feelings out of her body and energy field.

Helene did all of this and found what worked best for her, describing those moments when she released volatility as "time well spent." Getting past angry barriers, Helene realized she was really hurting and the anger was a cover for tremendous sadness.

Another unsuccessful IUI came and went. Her reactions were less angry. Instead, she became proactive and retained an adoption attorney to proceed with her Plan B. Helene also moved on from individual counseling to a fertility-focused mind-body workshop group to learn meditation techniques. Because a majority of her anger had been released, her headspace was cleared such that she could benefit from attempting peaceful techniques. Before, those techniques would have likely only resulted in headaches.

One more IUI resulted in disappointment, but with adoption as her back up plan, she was less angry than before. She proceeded to do IVF with PGD (pre-genetic determination) to screen out the embryos that were abnormal. Surprisingly, seven of nine embryos looked good. She had benefitted from practicing mind-body techniques combined with acupuncture. The transfer date fell on the anniversary of her mom's death. She thought it was a sign so she remained optimistic.

A chemical pregnancy resulted. She felt numb and hopeless. How could she keep going after so many false starts and heartaches?

Meditation, acupuncture, new friends who understood, and a new attitude helped her recover enough to use her remaining frozen embryos, which also failed to result in pregnancy. She finally reached her limit and surrendered. She told me that she was D-O-N-E, done. That day was to be her last acupuncture session.

I wished her well and understood her resignation. She had truly done everything. Helene was not mad anymore. She was at peace. The adoption proceedings, while not her first choice, allowed her to experience some forward movement in the direction of her goal of motherhood. She assured me she would stay in touch.

Five months later, a few months before her thirty-seventh birthday, Helene reappeared at the office. She said she had never felt such feelings of *detachment*... As adoption loomed closer and was becoming a very likely outcome, she felt her body could do one last IVF. That last cycle was different from all the others. There were no modifications to her IVF protocol, but there were huge noticeable changes in her.

Helene, who had suffered from constipation for most of her life, had been having regular movements every day for months. This was a physical confirmation that she was no longer "holding onto" anger. She also stopped wasting her acupuncture treatment time comparing herself to other people or criticizing pregnant celebrities. She really was at peace now. The anger was gone. She could open her heart to a baby. It was outwardly obvious that she had truly let it all go.

The cycle went slowly. Her body did not race through the stimulation phase and become hyper-stimulated as before. She appreciated having the financial resources and a body healthy enough to do IVF so many times. Determined to "graduate" infertility, she and her doctor opted to transfer back all of the embryos that passed PGD screening. Without anger blocking her second heart, she was able to fully invest herself emotionally and was going for it. Not surprisingly, this was the time she conceived. Twins! Two healthy twin boys, who made it all the way to thirty-seven weeks and weighed over seven pounds each.

Because she genuinely released her attachment to angry feelings, Helene could fully enjoy her boys and her future. She no longer felt the need to use anger to protect her heart from the things that happened in her past. She was, at last, truly liberated from the angry nature that once defined her.

Part 3

Say YES! to the Process of Becoming a Mother

Chapter 25

Practice Forgiveness

I have had patients who were unknowingly blocking their fertility by hanging onto hurt feelings. Maybe they were angry with their doctors, their husbands, or themselves. Perhaps their doctor over-stimulated their ovaries, causing them to delay a cycle and "waste" a crop of follicles; or they felt as if their husbands weren't involved enough in the effort to have a baby.

Oftentimes, a woman blames herself for having waited too long before getting started, or for choosing abortion in her earlier years. While blaming ourselves or resenting other people can give us a direction in which to send our negative energy, it doesn't allow for any personal growth. When we take responsibility for the role we play in our pain we actively participate in our healing by choosing to forgive, to let go, and release resentment or blame. By choosing this transformative path, we give ourselves the gift of an open heart and, subsequently, an open uterus. When we forgive, we become free from the pains of the past, and allow ourselves to participate in what is happening right now.

Blaming gets us nowhere. It only serves to further stagnate our energy by generating pathological emotional heat and more stagnation. Instead, we can choose to check inside and find our role in our demise. When we feel stuck is when we need to ask, "Am I over-giving again to friends and family and leaving too little for myself? Am I eating too much sugar? Staying up too late? What is the lesson for me right now that I am resisting?"

Being mad at ourselves and others definitely will not bring FSH down or bring your hormones into balance. Being mad that we lost a child will not bring them back. Being afraid that we've done irreversible damage to our eggs solves nothing. On the contrary, accepting personal responsibility, forgiving ourselves and recommitting to our motherhood dream, reveals self-love and healthy self-esteem. Practicing forgiveness can turn the table of infertility back in our favor.

The people I know who are unable to forgive face constant disappointment, frequent opposition, heartache, and continuous struggle. Universal Law suggests that *whatever we think about expands.* Describing our lives in terms of the ways we feel victimized or hurt usually generates more victimization and hurt in the future.

When we portray ourselves as victims of other people or circumstance, we lose all our power. On the path to motherhood, we cannot afford to waste our energy hanging onto old wounds inflicted by someone else or because of a life situation. Allowing forgiveness to deliver us from anger and resentment to a place of compassion and soft-heartedness is a much more open, fertile mindset.

As spiritual beings having a human experience, we often encounter great pain and trauma, which makes forgiveness seem impossible. It takes tremendous courage to forgive the unforgivable. It also requires a willingness to take responsibility for our role in the situation. If we can take as much as 1% responsibility for the things that have gone wrong in our lives, it will help us move towards forgiveness more readily, and get us unstuck.

That acknowledgment may be your first step toward true healing. Forgiving someone does not condone or un-do what has happened. Instead, forgiveness frees you from some of the pain that resulted from that injury, and allows you to move on with your life.

We all get hurt sometimes. We will all feel hurt again in the future, because facing pain in life is unavoidable. How we choose to recover from painful experiences is what defines our character and ultimately determines our destiny.

Making Peace with Tragedy

Eva was a returning patient who had used my acupuncture services and IVF to conceive her daughter a few years earlier. When she reappeared, I assumed it was because she wanted a sibling. It turned out she did want another daughter—because her first drowned in their pond.

Eva's baby's death was purely accidental. It was a case of the parents thinking the baby was with the nanny, and the nanny thinking the baby was with the parents. It was a tragic story that could have been prevented. After five failed IVF attempts, Eva came back in for acupuncture—eager to try anything that might help her conceive again.

I took a chance at helping to turn this sad story around. I suggested the *Grief Recovery Handbook* by John James and Russell Friedman. Recommending the book for guidance, I advised her to write a letter to her deceased eighteen-month-old daughter. I suggested that, in the letter, she forgive her daughter for wandering off; forgive herself for unknowingly being negligent, and forgive the nanny for being negligent, as well. Even though the event was an accident, she needed to attempt to get some closure and resolution. Otherwise, her body simply would not know what to do with the mess of conflicted emotions.

Eva found the courage to write the letter. It brought tears to my eyes when she read it to me at the office. She returned the following week to say that her heart felt open again. I did not hear from her until a few months later, when she showed up unexpectedly to tell me she was twelve weeks pregnant! She said she was looking forward to the future, and felt at peace with the past. That didn't mean she no longer missed her baby girl, but she recognized that being able to forgive created an opening for new life.

Are there old hurts and losses in your life that need to be forgiven in order to open your heart and uterus? Do you feel ready to release resentment from past wounds, if there is a chance it can change your life, and possibly improve your fertility? See if you can forgive yourself for having structural infertility, for waiting too long, or for putting your career goals first. Find the courage to experience the freedom that comes with being able to forgive.

Chapter 26

Become an Empowered Self-Advocate

This book is intended to stretch your mental capacity and motivate you to move beyond your perceived limitations into a place of personal wisdom and power. All the concepts mentioned thus far provide insightful ways to reframe infertility according to your individual needs. Incorporating these ideas has the potential to change a woman's fertility for the better while affecting many other areas of her life, as well.

We all face difficult times and fall short of our goals or act in ways that are less than our best. When my patients report that they are disappointed in themselves, or when they begin blaming themselves for another cycle that hasn't resulted in pregnancy, I remind them to reframe the situation. I ask them to see themselves, and their circumstances, from a new, more evolved perspective.

Instead of placing blame somewhere, I suggest they go within and ask themselves, "What can *I* do to improve my situation?"

Women who adopt this perspective become "empowered self-advocates." These are the women who *want* to learn about themselves. These women enjoy stretching and strengthening, seeing what they are made of, facing each new experience with curiosity instead of dread. They read empowering spiritual books and apply the knowledge directly to their lives. They look within to see where they are failing themselves or standing in their own way.

Not afraid to ask questions, these are the women who keep practitioners on their toes by actively participating in their fertility process; they volunteer information at appointments. These are the women who insist their doctor include them in decision-making. They find ways to establish mutually respectful relationships with their doctors, so they can feel safe to express concerns about their protocols.

Working with women who know themselves may take a little longer during intakes, as they have more information to share from their self-exploration. But they give their doctors valuable information about what they believe is working and what they might need to move forward. In doing so, a situation is set up for an attentive doctor to notice a subtlety or consider a different protocol that may work better.

Sometimes a little introspection, confidence, and the ability to think "outside the box," is what it takes to turn an average woman into an empowered, fertile woman who will go on to become a mother and gain the most amazing perspective from having grown through her experience.

Becoming Her Own Advocate

Christine, the thirty-nine-year-old woman mentioned in the Introduction of the book, began our relationship by showing me a very intimate photo from her recent wedding at her first acupuncture appointment. She shared that her powerful personality and passionate emotions had overwhelmed other men in her life. She was fiery and direct with her new husband as well, but he was secure enough in himself to appreciate the strength of her character, and encouraged its full expression.

For years she worked in the stressful entertainment industry, putting in long hours, and constantly tapping into her creative reserves to make documentary films. While the work fulfilled her on a professional and creative level, the long hours and stress left her with a combination of hormonal deficiencies, specifically depleting her adrenals and thyroid.

When I met Christine, she had an elevated FSH reading and symptoms related to decreased estrogen. She suffered endlessly from insomnia, headaches, hot flashes, and anxious agitation. Because of her age and elevated FSH status, she had already decided to proceed with IVF when we met. Our task was to prepare her as much as possible to make it a success.

I enjoyed Christine's powerful personality and appreciated the level to which she knew herself. I was impressed to see she had been charting her basal body temperatures and recording the positions of her cervix, gathering useful information and cultivating a fearless relationship with herself on that intimate level. This was not a woman afraid to pay attention to changes in her body, and she certainly demonstrated a commitment to do whatever would be necessary to become a mom.

We talked about her thyroid medication, wondering if her current dose was adding to her agitated state, and we initially used some herbs to help her sleep. They helped somewhat, but once her IVF protocol was underway, she stopped herbs and relied on the acupuncture alone to deal with the side effects of Lupron.

Despite her elevated FSH, Christine produced an impressive six follicles, with one embryo implanting and resulting in pregnancy. Unfortunately, her fetal hormone level did not stay elevated and she miscarried. This miscarriage, although emotionally painful, ended up being the perfect trigger for her to step into her power and seize the opportunity to get attempt to get pregnant naturally, relying on her own vast amounts of wisdom about her body collected along her particular journey.

Christine was a quick study and had closely observed the way her body reacted to each step of her IVF protocol. She already knew how she felt with too much or too little thyroid hormone. She knew that she responded well to the addition of estrogen and progesterone and that Lupron suppression made all of her deficiency symptoms much worse. She also knew from her BBT charting when she was most fertile and she knew that she had to surrender some old emotional patterns. She believed that she could figure out the way to her children and she was not going to let a miscarriage or a self-diagnosed case of the "Why me's?" get in her way!

Rather than staying obsessed with the knowledge of having elevated FSH, she reframed that and focused on the new information she had of how *well* she responded to supplemental hormones. Christine let that information guide her to a naturopathic physician, who prescribed bioidentical hormones. Using her body's clues and her internal wisdom, she alone decided how much to use and when she needed to apply her creams.

She sought spiritual guidance at her temple, uniting one afternoon with like-minded women who included her in a nurturing, healing ceremony. She then scheduled a session with the highly revered Maori Healers of New Zealand, and she came to Well Women Acupuncture an average of three times per week. Christine said the treatments helped her sleep better at night, which stabilized her mood swings, and that our consultation time before acupuncture provided an outlet for her thoughts. I was invited along to be a supportive ally in this process by keeping her encouraged and positive.

Closer and closer she came to a hormonally healthy and balanced state. On an emotional level, she healed her old wounds and started living in the present moment, turning passionate emotions and anxiety about getting pregnant into an exuberant joy for living her life with a fantastic husband.

Around the holidays that year, our office closed for a two-week break. She admitted having a brief feeling of trepidation to let that much time pass between her acupuncture sessions, but she had moved into such a place of surrender that it felt okay to her. As Christine said goodbye to me at the door, we joked about how she was ovulating and needed to get home right away. I said to myself, "I will hear from her with good news that she's pregnant on New Year's Day." And that is exactly what happened. She conceived her little girl possibly a few hours after we spoke!

At forty-one-years-old, quite by accident while nursing their ten-month-old daughter, she conceived a son... without any creams, supplements, doctors, or healers!

Chapter 27

Allow The Right One

Working with thousands of women has proven to me time and again that marrying "the right person" is on par with "getting to baby." Both usually involve the difficult task of surrendering, and accepting that the entire process cannot be forced. It has to be allowed to unfold and resolve itself in its own time.

Asking worried women to recall how they came to know their partners were "the one" for them is a source of great relief for me, because it never fails to restore the women's hope and trust. Anxiety ceases momentarily — as these women remember that it all came together for them in the end... as couples. They eventually got to the goal, despite serious kinks to work out beforehand.

If you are in a committed relationship, think for a moment about your own love story and how you came about calling in the right person for you. If you are not in a relationship, review how you approached trying to manifest a partner before ultimately deciding to start a family on your own.

Often the challenges surrounding fertility are the same hurdles women overcome while dating. The same patterns, limiting belief systems, and trust issues will be tested when trying to conceive. A woman will once again need to remember to trust that the right *child* for her will come at the right time.

Honest women in partnerships will admit they didn't do anything spectacular to get their partner. They trusted and let it all happen, despite how nervous they may have been, particularly in the beginning. When they go back in time and remember this, their attitude changes from panic and anxious thoughts of "Motherhood is never going to happen for me," to greater serenity. They remember, "Oh, yeah. We *did* go through some stuff before it all worked out. But it's better than I would have expected."

I have regularly asked my patients what was going on in their lives right before their intended person showed up. What were the conditions when obstacles were lifted and they were allowed to head steadfastly in the direction of commitment? Without fail, the women admit they found some degree of detachment, trust, and willingness to accept where they were in their lives, with or without a partner. They were also able to maintain a strange sense of certainty that it would turn out fine for them.

Women who feel secure enough to parent alone often have the same level of detachment, self-acceptance, courage, and faith.

Coupled or single women who have done significant personal development work end up being the ones most likely to pull off having a baby when odds are stacked against them. When facing significant challenges, these are the people who are able to appreciate what they have (partners, trusted friends and family) and can see the situation as an opportunity for growth.

Never have I heard of a successful union or family that resulted from one person forcing it to happen. Instead, I have witnessed the way healthy people behave during some of the most heartbreaking moments in their lives, demonstrating their resilience and character. From this place of personal strength, they take risks, try their best, and allow good things to come to them in time and in response to their efforts.

The best supporting advice I can give women who feel like they are doing all that and still baby has eluded them, is suggest they take a long look at themselves. Whatever energy they are putting out is what other people feel from them. That includes unborn babies still in their spirit form. Like encountering a soul mate, your baby and your family will result from a meeting of properly matched energies. It requires a mutual readiness and a collision of spiritual paths, all at the right time. The process seems to speed up when we detach a little and allow the various souls intended to meet you to do just that.

Aligning with Her Intended Baby

Kerin was referred to me by her reproductive endocrinologist, Dr. Kelly Baek. Dr. Baek made a point of phoning me about the referral of this single woman, because the two women knew each other from high school. We agreed to work as a team to get Kerin to her baby as quickly as possible.

When Kerin arrived I thought, "Hmm, this may not happen as easily as the doctor hopes." Kerin was thin, even slightly underweight, by what I consider optimal fertility standards. She was also a vegan. She would not eat any animal products at all, including eggs or milk. Kerin explained that she was committed to her vegan lifestyle "for spiritual reasons." Besides that, she just did not digest animal products well.

She was a successful forty-one-year-old advertising manager who would be doing this alone, raising the baby with her parents' love and full emotional support.

Her disposition was incredibly optimistic. I took it at first to mean that she had not read much about success rates and the infertility "epidemic." But as I learned in working with her for a full year, she was just a woman who liked her life. She could be optimistic, because a baby was going to be a bonus in her life. She enjoyed a full career, social life with fun friends, yoga classes at the beach, quiet weekends, regular visits with family, and she had two well-cared-for cats!

The first cycle involved an IUI. She came into the office for needles following the insemination, then prepared for her life to change two weeks later.

That was not the case, nor did it work the next time, or the next few cycles that included ovarian stimulation. Finally, she was advised to try IVF so they could see what the embryo quality looked like.

The doctor was taken aback when the embryologist reported that all of Kerin's embryos had literally disintegrated in the culture. They were so fragmented that Kerin was advised to pull out of ART completely for the time being, to give her body some rest and attempt another cycle in six months. Kerin's doctor and I discussed this case a few times, enough for us to agree that Kerin needed to address her restricted diet.

Because Dr. Baek was familiar with the success rate of the Well Women Acupuncture office and my fertility workshop, known as The Seed Fertility Program, we agreed to re-examine our approach and see what else could be recommended for Kerin to have a successful outcome. I made the suggestion that Kerin add animal products into her diet to put on some extra weight and naturally increase her estrogen supply.

We agreed and hoped that ultimately this would help her improve her egg quality. Because of Kerin's vegan status, Dr. Baek thought it would be best if she, as the medical doctor and her referring physician, made the professional suggestion that Kerin follow the dietary instructions exactly as outlined in my Seed Program, which recommends consuming unpasteurized milk and cage-free eggs.

Reluctant at first, Kerin decided to give it a chance. After all, a lot of money was put into those embryos that had been so fragmented, not to mention her time and effort. She was now completely invested in becoming a mother. She would try the milk and eggs.

She was surprised at how good the milk tasted, and how great she felt when she included it in her daily routine! Because the milk had its enzymes intact, she digested it just fine.

As for the eggs, she was not thrilled, but she committed to having two per day. She bulked up her diet, consulted a natural health practitioner for some advice on supplements, increased her workout regimen, and kept her weekly acupuncture appointments. Kerin also continued laughing with friends and spending time with her family.

The months passed and a sexier, curvier Kerin emerged. She knew she was more fertile. It was undeniable. The ultrasound at the six-month mark proved it was true, she had far more follicles to work with.

One more IVF produced much better eggs, but not a viable pregnancy. She took a month to rest, respecting her body's need to recover and recharge in between stimulation protocols. All the while, she stayed committed to her new diet and new lifestyle. After that resting month, she returned for a scan to find she had more eggs than ever, and Dr. Baek thought they looked perfect for a round of IVF. Kerin felt completely ready.

She conceived that time and her embryos showed little, if any, fragmentation. Her pregnancy persisted, as she passed every genetic test and sailed through an effortless pregnancy, delivering at age forty-three.

Kevin was born on Valentine's Day, and he is the embodiment of Kerin at her best. He is charming, handsome, and confident—worth every bit of extra effort and clearly "the one" for her.

Chapter 28

Redefine the Roles of the Egg and Sperm

I am frequently asked if we treat men in the office. We are trained first as general practitioners and, as such, we treat back pain, stress, stomachaches, and insomnia. Those ailments are common to all people. Our primary focus, however, is to lead and support women along a path to self-acceptance. But I always agree to treat the husbands of the Well Women patients, because it's a great way to help the women feel more supported. Oftentimes, we find the men are as greatly in need of support as their wives.

Sometimes these prestigious, career-focused women, who have taken on more "masculine" roles at work, carry that energy over into their relationships. The result is that the husbands or partners begin to feel emasculated. This typically works against baby-making efforts, unless there is a very healthy man on the other side of the equation who is completely secure in himself and the relationship.

In Chinese medicine, any predominance of yin (female) or yang (male) energy causes imbalance. Yin and yang are considered to be "interdependent," meaning you cannot have one without the other. They always come in a pair, like two sides of a coin.

Women planning to be single moms by choice, read carefully here; this chapter applies equally to you. Doing it alone requires effort on your part to balance your yin and yang, in an attempt to optimize your baby-making effort.

The yin, or female energy, is the part of us that reveals our receptivity.

It is open, vulnerable, and responsive, rather than aggressive and insistent. Remember previous chapters on patience and trust: The egg is a wise, but passive, force. Her "job" is to wait patiently before making her way down to the womb.

Conversely, sperm represent the yang counterpart. With their heads and tails, they provide the action component of this pairing. They race up through the vaginal canal, into the uterus, and inside the tubes. The sperm's role is to find the egg and provide the genetic material that merges with hers to make a new person. The itinerary for the female energy is: relax, rest, receive, wait. The male's mission is all about action: race in, provide what is needed, and make it happen.

We must be aware of how we balance our masculine energy with our feminine. We have to revel in the beauty, creativity, and receptivity of the feminine while being able to utilize our masculine that keeps us moving forward. The *balance* of the two is what allows peace and harmony to exist in our relationship with ourselves, as well as our intimate partners.

Just think what could be possible in our relationships if we started thinking in terms of blending our complementary energies. In every partnership one person embodies more yin energy, while the other person embodies more yang. Relationships work best when the partners complement each other. They tend to fall apart when there are two partners trying to occupy the same space.

People on a spiritual path are aware that they contain both yin and yang aspects within themselves. They recognize that healthy people are *whole* people—complete and fulfilled being outside of relationship. But in successful partnership with another, there is typically an understanding and division of the two roles, suggesting balance needs to be established to indicate who is more yin, and who is more yang within the relationship. Then it can work most effectively.

We see many successful, accomplished, important women coming into the office. But they are exhausted. They don't realize how much easier their lives could be, and possibly how much their fertility could improve, by simply pulling back on some of their masculine "out thrusting" behaviors.

For a couple going through ART, the husband's contribution seems comparatively small. It appears he gives a sample one morning and that's it. Beyond providing that vial of sperm, his ability to control the outcome is zero, rendering him powerless over his wife's happiness. This is not a powerful position for him to be in as a man.

The way to help him be his most masculine self (and perhaps improve sperm count/quality) is to embrace your vulnerability and share that with him. Women in same-sex relationships, or those going through the process alone need to do the same to maintain balanced energy in this process. Consider sharing your vulnerable feelings and fears with partners and trusted people in your life.

All women going through infertility can benefit from revealing how vulnerable it feels to endure countless vaginal ultrasounds, attend numerous acupuncture sessions, face one blank stick after another cursed blank stick, all the while knowing the pressure of family building resides on the receptivity of their "second heart." Understanding these newly defined aspects of our selves within our relationships is a healthy internalized process (yin) that, when expressed to others, typically generates a warm hug (yang).

Balance of Yin and Yang Energies

This couple worked alongside each other in their real estate office. Laura was admittedly guilty of micro-managing Dave's every move and criticizing his approach. She was always stressed that he was going to cause a mistake the minute she left him alone. Obviously, this was creating a power struggle, so I was not surprised to hear he had a reduced sperm count (from the unconscious but constant emasculation), which created a need for IVF.

Their IVF protocol included ICSI (surgical injection of one selected sperm into the egg), suggesting there was no need for Dave to get acupuncture or other treatments to increase his count. When Laura asked if I would treat him in the Well Women office for stress, I said "absolutely!" I was excited about the potential to facilitate a more harmonized balance between the yin and yang aspects of their relationship.

When I met them together, it was easy to see the love and chemistry between them. But the constant berating of his work style, combined with his diagnosis of inadequate sperm, was taking a toll on his self-esteem. To start, I suggested that the two of them schedule their appointments at different times, to allow each to feel they were in a safe space. As luck had it, Laura's MD recommended she take time off from work. This allowed her to get acupuncture, while he got the chance to work alone at the office. At this point, Laura was forced to surrender the control and let him handle things.

In her sessions, we peeled off layers of her tough exterior that were covering up an angry relationship with her past and a fear that, if she did not control everything at the office, her future would be awful, as well.

Dave's sessions were a chance for me to ask him about the ways he was succeeding at the office while Laura was at home. He was exhilarated! The more tired he was from working so much, the more powerful he felt as a man. It was stressful, but he loved the challenge to prove himself. It was helpful for him to have a time and place where he could boast his accomplishments.

I used their individual sessions to illustrate to both of them how well things were going at the office in Dave's hands. This not only highlighted the sustainability of what they had mutually created, but clearly demonstrated his ability to step up to the task of being a provider, as well. His effort deserved recognition, especially as all the attention was being placed on her for the upcoming IVF.

The irony was, although it was not necessary for their protocol, this man's sperm count actually *increased*, presumably from the acupuncture sessions. This gave him an additional new feeling of male power just in time for the egg retrieval. Putting the responsibility to provide back on Dave had actually helped their situation. Their doctor was impressed and Dave clearly appreciated feeling like a more powerful man.

As he continued to guide their business towards success, not only did Laura gain trust in him, but she also could finally relax and receive his contributions to their mutual goal of building a family.

It was sweet to watch, and as a result of their combined effort, they now have a little boy, who was conceived during that cycle in which they both focused on balancing the male energy between them.

Chapter 29

Express Gratitude

What's a chapter on gratitude doing in a book about surviving infertility? You may be thinking, "Until my baby gets here, how can I be *grateful* for all this disappointment, frustration, expense, and the hassles of trying and trying again, only to have my self-confidence beaten down?"

A huge part of our success as Well Women acupuncturists has come from having the extraordinary ability to help women find things to be grateful for along this arduous journey. We help them see that there really are things to appreciate *now* – not just when they succeed at becoming a mom.

I start by asking my patients these questions: What is working in your life? In what areas do you have abundance? What leaves you feeling joyous and full of wonder? Also, what lessons have you learned from the difficult parts of this process? List these things on paper, or consider starting a gratitude journal.

When I ask women what they are most grateful for, the first and most common response is a sense of thankfulness for their partners and family. Despite sometimes being emotional punching bags, these people remain the relentless keepers of faith for us on this path. They miraculously know what to do or say when nothing else is of any comfort. They console, uplift, and support. Sometimes they fearlessly administer painful hormone injections or loan us the money to do an expensive cycle.

These loving people who have listened tirelessly to your fertility struggles, who helped you find the strength within yourself to keep going— think of how grateful you are for them. Their helpful energy and thoughtful prayers really do make a positive difference. This lengthy journey to motherhood provides several opportunities for you to see just how much love surrounds you.

Next, can you find some appreciation for having the opportunity to participate in some of the most exciting experimental medicine ever? Sometimes I wonder if women are giving any thought to the medical miracles these doctors are facilitating. The ability to manipulate our tiniest and most important cells, to time it all so perfectly as to result in the formation of *another human being...* is out of this world!

Finally, women attempting to get pregnant could also benefit from finding more appreciation for what their bodies are accomplishing during each cycle. Each fertility attempt asks the ovaries to work incredibly hard, trying to get baby here. Instead of maturing one follicle per month naturally, with ART there can be as many as three, six, twelve, sometimes over twenty follicles stimulated in an attempt to make the one that will survive the vulnerability of high-tech manipulation procedures to become your child.

Inserting a little more gratitude and appreciation for all the attempts your body has made could make a difference in your outcome. Perhaps expressing an occasional thought like, "Thank you, body, for trying so hard to give me this dream..." could help your situation by triggering more self-love and acceptance of this path.

Over the years, my friends have marveled at my ability to work at the level of emotional intensity that I do, sustaining the long hours and incredible tension of sitting with women as they struggle with uncertainty, pain, and disappointment. The friends who know me best also know my personal life left much to be desired, as they watched me survive breakups and contend with the demands once placed on me by my mother.

However, it is these extraordinary circumstances for which I am the most grateful. During these times I grew the most as a spiritual person, and the patients keep me propelled along my spiritual path towards greatness!

I am forever indebted to them for bringing their broken hearts to me and trusting in our combined intention to make a positive shift occur for them.

It is easy to be grateful when things are going our way, but that is not when we grow. Just as the lotus flower grows from the silt and minerals in the muddy bottom of a pond, if we look carefully, using an open heart and an open mind, we can always find something to be thankful for. Attempting to do so keeps this fertility journey and its obstacles in perspective, while bringing to light the fact that our lives are already full of wonderful gifts. It is up to us to start looking with more grateful eyes.

Finding Gratitude in an Unenviable Situation

Thirty-one-year-old Shantelle and her fifty-eight-year-old fiancé Joe had good reason to believe IVF would be necessary to get pregnant. They faced a combination of potential fertility obstacles: decreased sperm quality and a prostate infection for him, while she had been diagnosed with polycystic ovaries and possibly a blocked fallopian tube. She also had a history of losing a baby two years prior, six weeks into the pregnancy.

When Shantelle came to our office, they were both taking antibiotics for his genitourinary infection. Their wedding was a few weeks away, and she was questioning her current doctor's urgent insistence that she head straight to IVF when their life was so unsettled. I sent her home with a list of specialists whom I considered the most respected reproductive endocrinologists in the area. I chose doctors for the couple who mutually respected the role of acupuncture in the process of ART.

I treated Shantelle that day for pre-wedding jitters. She returned two weeks later, having a completely different and more relaxed treatment plan set up with one of our referral doctors. She was confident, excited, and now prepared for her wedding and insemination instead of IVF.

The next time I saw her she was married and seven weeks pregnant! Her situation, however, was nothing to envy. Shantelle, this savvy attorney, had just unknowingly become married to a pathological liar who was addicted to sex, prostitutes, and alcohol. Within days after their wedding, a complete exposé of his trysts and outlets for self-loathing were revealed.

Can you imagine a better example of a reason to be angry, ungrateful, or disappointed? Shantelle really embodied a "Stick It to Me, Baby!" disposition, because although now she was pregnant, she suddenly had to face the likely dissolution of her marriage. Previously, she only had the frustration of trying to get pregnant. Now she would have to attempt to transform all of her disappointment into an opportunity for happiness. Was it even possible?

At each session, she came in with new despicable information about her husband's secret life, but managed to speak compassionately on his behalf. Not condoning or accepting of his behavior, she instead was able to express gratitude beyond words that she had a healthy baby growing inside of her! Despite nausea and vomiting, back pain and lack of sleep from pregnancy and stress, she maintained such a spiritually graceful and empowered attitude about her situation.

Immediately, the couple sought the help of twelve-step programs, but unsuccessfully. This man had so little respect for himself that he skipped the agreed upon meetings and counseling sessions. He continued lying, sneaking off with other women, and sabotaged every attempt made to reconcile.

Shantelle turned to her father and brothers for support. She felt safe to confide in them and looked to them as examples of honorable men. They provided her with reminders of who she was and how strong and whole she was as a woman. They reassured her that she would be a terrific mother who would always have their support and masculine contribution to the child's life, if necessary. They restored her sense of trust that everything would be fine eventually, by reminding her to return to her spiritual and religious roots for answers about what to do.

What impressed me most about Shantelle was her irrepressible sense of gratitude for her unborn baby and her healthy pregnancy. Throughout her ordeal, she remained completely grateful for the opportunity to be a mother to this long-awaited child.

I spoke to her many months later, when her son Matthew (whose name means: "Gift from God") was three months old. He was strong and healthy. She was reveling in her new role as a mother, describing the feeling as unlike anything she could have ever imagined. This feeling of loving another human being so completely and unconditionally sometimes took her breath away.

When I asked about her marriage, she said she was grateful for all the lessons the experience taught her. On her gratitude list was our office—because we led her to the right doctor. We also helped her emotionally get through the initial shock of her husband's news. Secondly, she was overcome with gratitude for the lesson of "selflessness" that only motherhood can provide.

She was clearly in a place of spiritual acceptance as she explained her recent life philosophy: "Nothing happens that is not supposed to happen." Stating that the ultimate lesson for her was to appreciate "it's not about being angry; it's about being an adult." Admittedly, forgiving was easier than forgetting, but she was already aware that her little boy was observing her every move. It was, therefore, of utmost importance she try her best to live a life of compassion, rather than holding on to ugly judgment and hatred for her husband.

Though Shantelle and Joe are no longer married, Matthew, this little gift from God, continues to facilitate his father's healing just by being a loving recipient of his dad's love. Watching Matthew grow and look to dad for guidance has provided Joe the chance (and good reason) to turn his life around.

Chapter 30

View Life as a Journey

What is the best part of going on a hike? Is it capturing the view at the top of a mountain? Or is it the process of taking each challenging step upward, perhaps with a treasured friend to share the experience? The answer to this question usually confirms our derived satisfaction and appreciation for triumphing over something difficult.

The view from the bottom up to the top of a mountain always looks cumbersome. Yet we believe, or have learned from experience, putting one foot in front of the other and moving forward will get us there eventually. Remembering that our lives are essentially one big journey that leads us towards greater spiritual evolvement can help us see that our day-to-day experience is filled with flat, beautiful trails *and* strenuous, uphill climbs. When we allow ourselves to understand that life is a spiritual journey, it becomes easier to find the faith necessary within ourselves to accomplish goals or survive our most challenging times. We gain trust in ourselves after we transcend those challenges.

All journeys involve some type of preparation, however, and the "fertility journey" is no different. To prepare physically, we need balanced hormones, properly thickened uterine lining, structural or energetic blockages removed, and genetically viable gametes. To prepare mentally, we need to give ourselves permission to feel peace and acceptance with the emotional trials inherent in the process of creating another human being.

One of the most emotionally difficult aspects of the journey is repeatedly surviving the challenging period following ovulation or embryo transfer. The luteal phase, otherwise known as the "Two-Week Wait," is sometimes referred to as a "detour into crazy town" because of the negative side effects many experience in response to elevated progesterone.

This two-week period is the time in which otherwise sensible, confident women lose belief in their ability to complete the journey, and they fall apart emotionally. They question everything they once believed to be good about themselves or their lives. This is the part of the journey I liken to the burn of an uphill climb; for sure, it is the hardest part of the cycle for nearly all the women I have worked with. This Two Week Wait is all about a success-or-failure mindset. The information you learn about yourself in these moments can serve your growth for the rest of your lifetime.

Remembering those parts of your life's journey in which you have succeeded (like having a career you love, or creating a home that impresses and reflects your style, or finding the right partner for you) will help you stay the course. Try to envision this uncomfortable time of your life as only a small part of your larger spiritual journey that will ultimately lead to inner peace and happiness.

Acknowledge how every person has arrived and every event has occurred at the right time in your life, for a specific purpose. The people you need along the way—teachers, lovers, guides, doctors, friends, and family—are all intended to help you grow into the person you are supposed to be. They all show up perfectly on schedule, even our children. The disappointments you have experienced are also perfectly designed and scheduled to strengthen you for what lies ahead.

Because my own journey continued alongside my patients, I started making the connections between the lessons I was learning (forgiveness, gratitude, patience, trust...) and the type of patient cases that came my way. With each woman, I had the opportunity to teach *and* to learn.

At some point in my journey, my dad (usually a man of few words) recommended I think of my life as a journey down a river. He reminded me life is nothing but a unidirectional current that leads, ultimately, to an ending. It will someday be the experience of taking the journey that will matter. Along the way, I would face rough rapids, as well as stretches of relaxed or swift, smooth currents.

I stopped viewing my journey as a continuous uphill, arduous hike. I started coasting for once, allowing this "river" to take me where it was going to; I no longer fought against its current. I still embraced the concept that life was a journey, but I set the intention to enjoy the totality of the journey and resist the urge to get stuck so frequently with life's inherent disappointments.

Just like a river or hiking trail presents unknown terrain, surprises and different routes before leading to an endpoint, a fertility journey does the same thing. Enjoying the process along the way will make your "view" at the end that much more rewarding, and possibly include the child who is waiting for you.

Two Different Women, Two Very Different Journeys

Both Kim and Hope had fertility journeys that led them to participate in a UCLA Mind-Body Institute workshop, in conjunction with Well Women Acupuncture treatments. Combining Mind-Body training with our unique acupuncture style helped both women understand the process of becoming a mother can require time, patience, physical pain, effort, and loss. Women who "work on themselves" using alternative methods may find themselves better prepared for the times when the journey does not lead to a baby.

After nearly two years of attempting various IUI's to get pregnant, thirty-six-year-old Kim opted for an IVF cycle. She had a frail constitution, a history of fibroids, insomnia, and heart palpitations from a congenital heart condition that caused irregular heart muscle contractions. From a Chinese gynecology perspective, she was a textbook example of a woman who would benefit from herbal supplementation to strengthen her heart blood.

Nourishing herbs strengthened her body and spirit and helped her sleep at night. She responded well to a formula intended to treat those issues, but her husband was averse to the idea of including further herbal therapy during her IVF protocol, so we relied on acupuncture and emotional healing to improve her chances of conception.

Despite being a small and delicate woman, her ovaries produced twenty-eight follicles during stimulation and yielded eighteen fertilized embryos! During the egg retrieval, her doctors noted cervical stenosis, a tightening of the cervical opening, which made the procedure more difficult. Her doctor concluded she would need to be anesthetized at the time of the embryo transfer to easily guide the embryos into her uterus.

She conceived with that initial cycle, but her delicate nature and fragile physical body reacted negatively to the procedures, leaving her to experience intense cramping and pelvic pain. A few weeks later, she was hospitalized for pregnancy-related hyperemesis (unrelenting vomiting) and dehydration. While she was in the hospital, the doctors found a blood clot located close to the fetus. Shortly after this discovery, Kim lost the baby and began hemorrhaging, which increased after her DNC. She lost one-half of her total blood volume and almost required a blood transfusion in order to survive.

Two months later, an extremely weakened Kim and her husband showed up for acupuncture. I was stunned to hear they were going to attempt another transfer with more of their frozen embryos, given how close she had come to losing her own life with the previous attempt. They wanted me to help her regain her strength to prepare for the next cycle. I reserved judgment, understanding they felt ready to become parents and knowing they, like so many of my patients, believed family building was an experience worth the risk.

It took three months for her to recover the weight she lost from her ordeal, and to regain the ability to walk a few steps without tiring. We recommended various forms of meat protein, greens, and "good" fats to help her regain strength. Her husband asked me to prepare a large refill of the Chinese herbs given months prior.

She waited almost four more months before the next IVF cycle. Kim was learning not to rush her body to recover, nor to force it to be ready before it was time.

Her first frozen IVF cycle did not result in pregnancy. Instead, it resulted in Kim learning to cultivate more patience along her journey. The second and third frozen cycles also did not result in pregnancy, but they interpreted this as a sign that it was time to work with a different doctor.

Her second doctor conducted a thorough antibody panel and found the likely cause of the initial blood clot in the first pregnancy. She would need steroids to prevent rejection of a fetus in future attempts. Kim found more trust and received more nurturing support from her new doctor, who performed a mock transfer in advance to see how Kim's tight cervix would respond on the big day.

Having acupuncture at the time of the embryo transfer allowed her to have her fourth frozen transfer without any anesthesia. She was much more relaxed in general. Her improved physical state was likely result of taking time to prepare her body and learning in advance what it would need if she conceived again.

Kim did conceive and from the start the doctor prescribed high amounts of fluid and more food intake long before nausea would become too much of an issue. She still had some nausea, but it was better managed. She was stronger and more prepared this time. Her pregnancy journey required complete bed rest from the beginning, but she listened to her body, and let it create her son in peace. Kim did not waste energy fighting or feeling scared. She just took each day one step at a time. She now has a very healthy and strong little boy.

Kim's story had a successful outcome. Their perseverance and courage were transformed into a healthy little being. How wonderful it is when everything eventually concludes nicely to make sense of the struggle and difficult parts of the journey.

However, as I have walked my own path as a spiritually-focused fertility acupuncturist, I have had to accept and help other women accept that not all persons seeking babies will successfully reach that destination. In these cases, the true understanding that life is about spiritual transformation is what awaits at the top of the fertility mountain.

Hope began acupuncture with me when she was thirty-five. Equipped with two years' worth of BBT charts and lab values, Hope's journey had already included six IUI's and a hysterosalpingogram (HSG), which revealed a blocked fallopian tube. Hope also had little or no cervical mucus. Thankfully, her ovaries didn't appear to be problematic; her FSH was only 6.4. But in addition to the other concerns, her husband's sperm analysis confirmed reduced motility.

Because of her age, her positive attitude, openness to try anything, and the advanced technology of IVF, I figured Hope would find her way to healthy pregnancy by the following spring.

Her first acupuncture treatment impressed her so much with respect to the power of alternative medicine to calm and relax her busy brain. She believed that she could benefit spiritually and psychologically from the subtle shifts in her energy field. Having such a positive response, she decided to spend time pursuing natural approaches before investing their entire life savings in IVF.

Of all the patients I have worked with, Hope's journey involved the most adventures. At each treatment, she would recount the various different pieces of information she was gathering about her body from her collective alternative therapies. It was fascinating.

She participated in the Mind-Body workshop, sought hypnotherapy, continued with her BBT charting, pumped her husband full of vitamins and supplements, used a turkey baster to inject actual egg whites she was told would mimic cervical mucus, and she indulged visualizations of herself with a healthy baby boy who grew to be a strong young man visiting with her in her kitchen. Hope wrote a letter saying goodbye to a previously aborted baby. All of this provided her with a sense of resolution from the past and instilled inspiration for her future.

After five months of alternative healing, she started inserting some of her sense of humor into her situation, thinking a lighter attitude would help her chance of success. She referred to herself as "an experiment," and continued her journey through the various alternative methods. She refused to stop collecting information and rejected any idea of giving up.

The next few months included trips to a chiropractor, consumption of daily wheatgrass juice, and Qi Gong practice. Hope participated in a controversial immunotherapy procedure (Lymphocyte Injection Therapy) that could only be done outside the United States. The procedure claimed to reduce her newly diagnosed immunoreactivity to her husband's sperm. Along the way, she learned she inherited a gene that coded for Thrombophilia, a serious blood-clotting tendency. So she researched more supplements for that, sought psychotherapy, a psychic advisor, and another acupuncturist.

Still working with me throughout this rollercoaster ride of alternative treatments, she opted to see my teacher, as well—per her psychic's advice and to satisfy the need to "cover all the bases."

Hope's journey continued as she added osteopathy, saliva, and hair analysis, a feng shui consultation, craniosacral therapy, and reflexology to a catalog of alternative routes intended to treat her growing list of immune and structural fertility blocks. She underwent laparoscopic surgery, which revealed severe endometriosis adhesions and cysts that blocked both her ovaries from successfully sending eggs to the tubes, and found her left tube was permanently damaged from scar tissue.

After this surgery, she proceeded to her first of three IVF attempts.

Her first IVF resulted in pregnancy! What a relief it was to see all her efforts rewarded. And what a tragedy it was to see her pregnancy, like Kim's, end in miscarriage at nine weeks due to a blood clot and hemorrhage.

The combination of exhaustion, loss, despair, and expense led Hope to stop everything she was doing. She needed to harness all the outpouring energy in order to consolidate herself.

Doing so helped her conceive a few more times—once more via IVF and twice naturally. Each time she miscarried she had to recover and sit with the poisonous empty feelings left inside. It appeared to be such a painful journey, especially since she was such a generous and kind-hearted spirit.

For a few years we kept in touch over the phone. The last time I talked to her, she had shredded all four years of her BBT charts, writing journals, and most of her immunology research. Hope and her husband moved out of the state. The last time I heard from her, she was forty-four-years-old and enjoying a new life, living on a ranch with dogs she raised as puppies and referred to as her four-legged children.

Sometimes a biological child is just not meant to come to us in this lifetime. What was important for Hope to move forward was the solace of knowing she applied herself 200% to creating the possibility of a baby happening for them. Her life is not full of regret, but rather, full of experiences that define who she is: a resolved woman who courageously walked through loss.

Chapter 31
Be Honest with Yourself

The decision to have a child is enormous, and may be overly influenced by the allure of pregnant bellies, tiny baby clothes, or the desire to keep up with our closest friends. Having a baby impacts every single aspect of life -- the life you may have worked hard to create; one of predictable comfort and personal liberties. Are you really ready to invite this big change? Could you inadvertently be blocking pregnancy by not wanting to admit the possible change actually terrifies you?

Sure, it is fun to imagine how cute your baby will be, what life will be like as a parent, or the romance of creating someone who is the embodiment of you and your life partner. However, if you are truly honest with yourself, you may admit being resistant to what your life will become; very little sleep, breastfeeding pressure, public diaper changing, a complete shift in your relationship, body changes, restricted freedom, and the profound responsibility of having a little person depend completely on you – for the next eighteen years and beyond.

This chapter is not intended to scare you or change your mind about having a baby. On the contrary, I hope it helps you be honest about your motivations. You may discover a truth that is hindering your fertility success. Or you may find honest reflection will be what inspires you to keep going despite disappointment.

Career women who identify with their successes sometimes aren't sure they are ready to trade it all for night feedings and temper tantrums at the grocery store. Many have hidden ambivalence, but due to family or other social pressure, feel the need to have a baby. You may be worried you do not earn enough to provide security, or question the longevity of your marriage. However, the fear of being denied something convention says you should want may have you convincing yourself you need to start a family, regardless.

Whatever the case, an honest self-assessment is crucial. Do you want a child because you are bored in your relationship? Do you feel it is time because everyone you know has a family? Maybe you just turned forty and your doctor or friends have told you age is now an issue. Perhaps you are motivated to have a baby because you think your first child needs a sibling.

Most people have an unspoken story running in the back of their minds; often a fantasy notion about a dreamy life with baby that is like walking into the sunset, forever happy. When people who want children compare this fantasy to the real lives they lead, they erroneously begin to create a story in which their lives are meaningless without a child. Add the side effects of hormone treatments for infertility or the heartache that compounds with miscarriages, and the real rollercoaster ride begins. Amid overcoming these obstacles, a couple may lose sight of why, or even if, they wanted a child in the first place.

Whether it's true or not, the stories we create spin around in our heads. I used to tell myself there was no room for a baby in my busy work schedule and life alone without a partner. After facing a series of breakups, I entertained a story that I was too sad and had too many odds stacked against me to have a family; being in constant service to others was to be my lot in life. Despite helping everyone else solve problems, I could not solve my own. Telling myself this sad story brought even more negativity into my life, until I looked deeper and realized there was no truth to what I was saying.

I made a conscious decision to let go of my fear-based stories of doom and gloom, realizing there was only truth in those statements if I gave them power. Instead I started saying, "I will be able to mother my child. My body is healthy enough to have a successful pregnancy. There is absolutely a good man somewhere on the planet who is intended to have a family with me." Once I started listening to my new story, knowing it was the truth, things changed.

This new story was entirely accurate. At age thirty-six, I heard from my former boyfriend Dan, the man I initially asked for sperm (when I wanted to prove my doctors wrong). Again, he offered me the chance to see if I could become pregnant, but this time I had different motivation. Watching so many women fervently pursue family building without thoughtfully exploring why they were doing it gave me the insight to honestly list all the reasons I wanted to be a mother. I could now say I wanted to have someone other than myself to focus on. I believed I had sufficient wisdom to pass on to children. I knew, honestly, I could nurture a child and take care of myself, as well. Before then, those same statements would not have been true.

Through forgiveness, understanding, and being honest about what it would mean to have a child with someone I knew to be a real person, not a perfect man from a fantasy, I was also able to tell myself the truth about why I would open myself to this man and this opportunity. He wanted to raise kids with me because he respected me; it was not about romance or some fairytale ideal. After a month of very long, very honest discussions, Dan and I concluded we both wanted the experience of child rearing enough to sacrifice certain personal freedoms and romantic notions.

This practice of honesty along the way also did something drastic inside my body that allowed us to conceive not just one, but two healthy babies, each with one natural attempt only. Rewriting my sad, fantasy-based story into a story of faith and truth paid off in the end.

Consider your own story and notice if you are telling yourself something true, or if you are cementing a false belief you have created in your mind out of fear, sadness, frustration, or repeated disappointment and loss. The stories a woman tells herself usually shed light on why she is not a mother yet. Vow to discover which parts of your history are true and worthy of sharing, and which can finally be discarded.

Writing a New Story as a Mom

Lexy was a beautiful thirty-six-year-old attorney who was referred to me early in my career as a fertility acupuncturist. Early or not, it was obvious at her first appointment why this woman had trouble conceiving naturally. She was not mean, but she was cold. She was curt, and strictly to the point with her answers to my questions. To thrive in her legal practice, she had learned to suppress her softer, feminine side in order to gain respect. This smart dresser with expensive taste had gone to drastic extents to be taken seriously, including having had breast reduction surgery. Upon meeting her, my first thought was, "What will she do when her baby spits up on that nice suit?"

Lexy had two failed IVF cycles before her doctor referred her to our office. After researching acupuncture, herself, she committed to giving it a try. She amazed me with her compliance in taking the Chinese herbs, stating she liked them so much she wanted to double her dosage, if possible. Her body was craving the nourishment apparently, as she was inclined to skip breakfast and lunch sometimes, waiting until 10pm to have dinner, with coffee or small snacks throughout the day.

I mentioned the effects of stress on women's ovaries, equating her skipping meals with the stress of being chased by a tiger. Lexy found my analogies interesting and she liked the soothing effects of acupuncture. What bothered her, she said, was my direct questioning about how she honestly planned to squeeze a baby into her already packed schedule, and if she was *really* ready to turn her life upside down.

Without much hesitation, she told me sharply I had just touched on the issue she feared most. She assured me she was working it out in therapy sessions, and all she wanted from me was my needles and what she had read about acupuncture: reduced stress and increased fertility.

"At least she is not lying to herself," I thought, and left my mother-hen questions out of her future sessions. The combination of needles, herbs, improved eating habits, relaxation, and IVF proved successful in getting her pregnant that cycle.

The fertilized embryo implanted in her fallopian tube, resulting in an ectopic pregnancy. The high level of fetal hormone in her system made her quite nauseated and tired; then she was prescribed chemotherapy medication to dislodge the growing embryo, which weakened her further.

Four months later, a softer, gentler, more emotionally open, and physically depleted attorney reappeared at the Well Women Acupuncture office.

"I'm still not in the mood to talk about it. But I am coming around and I am closer to being ready to be a mom," she announced honestly, without my prompting.

The ectopic pregnancy provided her the chance to give pregnancy and motherhood a serious consideration. In those few short weeks before the pregnancy ended, she was forced to confront her fears and change her story. The loss humbled and softened her, and made her more willing to look honestly at her behaviors and attitude about motherhood.

Her next cycle was the one that finally brought her son into the world. The pregnancy crippled her with fatigue and nausea, which forced her to work less, eat more regularly, and put more focus on nurturing herself. The impending responsibilities of motherhood were turning out to be good for her in many unexpected ways already.

This woman was aware all along of the story she was telling herself: that she needed to be successful and powerful, better than her own parents had been. The trouble was, her story was false; "successful, powerful, and perfect" are three words not found in the definition of mother. The stressful, long hours she kept at work to achieve that goal hindered her fertility and created a need for expensive IVF protocols.

Lexy started telling herself a different story: that she would be able to maintain her status as a powerful attorney who worked hard—and she could be a terrific mother. She had to come to terms with her beliefs, but when she did, her story changed. The last time I spoke to Lexy, she was happily working part-time as an attorney, and full-time as a mom. She does not miss her old way of being, which was goal-oriented and driven by the need to succeed. Instead, she defines her life as a true success story, in which she gained respect for accomplishments made in both her "careers"!

Chapter 32

Let Your Heart Overflow

Chinese gynecology teaches that women can conceive when the "kidney essence is abundant, the heart blood is overflowing, and sperm meets egg." However, depression and long-standing grief from continuous failed fertility attempts depletes both blood and essence. According to the Chinese classics, kidney essence naturally begins to decline for all woman over the age of thirty-two. Fertile outcomes viewed from this perspective seem bleak and unlikely.

I was thirty-two when I heard this information, and had already been diagnosed with threatening fertility problems. Knowing full well the universe or God brings us exactly what we need, I was not surprised when Alison Armstrong of PAX Programs entered my life. Alison's teachings empower women by showing them how to improve their relationships with men. In a second workshop, she exposed the fact that most women are operating from a place *far* from overflowing; she brought the room to tears as she illuminated how most women are operating at "near empty" most of the time.

While she applied her findings to the often frustrating dynamic between men and women, I applied the information to women's struggles with fertility, linking her "near empty" to "deficient qi and blood."

The women I work with are typically happily married, but they have such trouble reaching their final goal of having a baby. I wondered if it was because they were relying on baby to fill what they thought was lacking in their lives.

Alison explained that we needed to perceive ourselves as a collection of "tanks." These tanks are viewed as repositories of certain spiritual characteristics (she calls them noble traits of the "Queen") we possess that can be supplemented or depleted each day in response to life choices. Other people can count on us to provide certain things when our tanks are full enough. If we can figure out what behaviors fill our tanks, then we would be responsible for maintaining a feeling of totality, wholeness, or happiness sufficient to have it spill over for others to enjoy.

I knew applying a similar version of Alison's methodology to my patients' lives would probably hold true and help increase the number of mothers in the world.

After benefiting personally from her wisdom about how to keep my own tanks full, I started helping my patients apply the same logic to their lives and found Alison's concept revolutionary.

Each woman I shared this idea with loved learning how to get her tanks filled. The intense responsibility they were putting on an unborn baby to fill them up lessened significantly. Just as Alison had intended, the women became more empowered at the mere prospect of being able to maintain their own overflowing heart.

A Different Meaning of Abundance

"So it seems that we have something in common," Ben said to me, pointing at my large belly in my first pregnancy. "My wife is pregnant, and I waited fifty-four years to know this sense of joy."

Ben is a distinguished and hugely successful real estate broker in my neighborhood. We were talking while eating breakfast at a local Mexican restaurant.

The restaurant owner had seen it fit to introduce the two of us on this day, knowing what I do for a living and what personal struggle Ben and his wife Keri had gone through recently. Normally this multi-millionaire sat quietly, talking to no one while eating breakfast quickly, before racing to his office to earn even more money. Today, however, he not only made time to talk to me, he shared the experience that had humbly brought him to his knees, as he said, "like nothing else."

Ben and Keri had way more money than they knew what to do with. After a year of doing fertility treatments, they realized a baby was the one thing their money could not buy. Their struggle with infertility made them rethink the meaning of abundance.

"It sounds like overflowing amounts of money and the interest in starting a family just is not enough these days," I volunteered. Having his full attention about this topic I find more interesting than anything else, I continued, "There must also be a spiritual *breakthrough* for people intended to be parents. There needs to be something that reveals the overflow of love coming from their hearts; sometimes it must be strong enough to commit to parenting someone else's child."

"That's what happened for me and my wife!" he exclaimed. "She's forty and we had tried three different doctors. Eventually I asked our doctor what makes couples stop trying. He said patients either run out of money, or they run out of hope. We had an abundance of both, but we opened up to the idea of using a donor's egg, because it was what required the least amount of drugs for my wife. We are so happy and so ready to love this child!"

Ben looked like he could cry; but instead he started sweating profusely, the kind of anxious sweat that comes from being completely vulnerable with a stranger about your most intimate life experience.

When infertility disappointment strikes again and again *and again*, it seems easier to just give up. However, it is often not possible to walk away from the innate feeling that parenting is your next big purpose in life. Here was this man, with more money than he could spend in one lifetime, yet he was unable to buy the happiness that comes from raising a child. The moment he and his wife understood this spiritual bent on infertility, they instinctively allowed all the hope they shared to flow into the process. Keri's donor-assisted pregnancy occurred effortlessly.

When our hearts have an overflowing abundance of love, we cannot help but share it with the world. The thought of loving a baby conceived via egg donor or through adoption or foster care seems very natural when we have extra love to give to another human being. The best part about having a spiritually-based perspective about family building is that our awareness of our abundance of love can be what allows love to be returned to us at last.

Hearts Broken... Open!

At her first appointment, a sweet thirty-three-year-old Kristen appeared to have it all. She came from a loving family with four sisters, had a teaching job she enjoyed, and a fantastic home she remodeled with her handsome fireman husband of four years, Jay. She also had uterine fibroids, very painful periods, irregular BBT charting patterns, varying cycle lengths suggesting questionable ovulation, and eighteen months of infertility frustration.

She became emotional as she described her battle with feelings of loneliness and isolation. Kristen was the only one of the five sisters unable to have children. She felt guilty, too, because her husband was the only fireman at the station who did not have a toddler to bounce around and carry on his shoulders.

Months of unsuccessful attempts resulted in a sperm analysis which revealed slight abnormalities in Jay's sperm. Meanwhile, her menstrual pain combined with dark, clotted, blood that had a mucus-like appearance, suggested a need for laparoscopy to diagnose and treat possible endometriosis.

Both Kristen and Jay started acupuncture. They both took Chinese herbs. His sperm quality improved, as did his back pain and stress level. Her periods improved with respect to pain level and blood quality. Still, she was not getting pregnant. In each acupuncture treatment, Kristen expressed love and appreciation for her sisters and shared how hard it was to connect with them only in sisterhood, but not through motherhood.

She started ART in much the same way so many other women do—with a few IUIs, followed by stimulated IUIs (which resulted in cysts, increased mood swings and more menstrual pain). Then came the lure of IVF. Her doctor wanted her to postpone laparoscopy, suggesting it would only be recommended if the IVF failed.

Believing something structural was preventing natural conception and possibly implantation, Kristen researched endometriosis with a passion. She worked with me to create a balanced, anti-inflammatory diet that would help her reproductive system and reduce the toxic effects of estrogen dominance and hormone imbalance that leads to endometriosis. She insisted on having a laparoscopy prior to IVF, but decided to incorporate moderate exercise and lifestyle changes to create the most ideally fertile environment, and hoped to conceive soon after the surgery.

She approached her healing methodically and strategically. Eliminating all forms of wheat and dairy and adding omega-three essentially fatty acids reduced her bloating and menstrual cramping to nearly zero, because she balanced the pain-inducing prostaglandin hormones that were coming in from her diet. For three months she got into the routine of avoiding foods that caused pelvic pain, and strengthened her body physically to prepare for the surgery.

Laparoscopy revealed stage-one and stage-two endometriosis on both of her ovaries. IVF was her most likely option to conceive, but now she knew for certain her body was inclined to turn inflammatory foods into pelvic adhesions. She was empowered with the knowledge.

As excited as she was about the upcoming IVF, she started having new emotional sensations she described as "heart-opening" feelings. She had joined a Mind-Body group and loved the sensation of being included in a different "sisterhood." The connections to these women helped her see she was not alone in her heartache and readiness to love a child. What was becoming clear to her was that she was ready to love another being; it did not need to be her own.

One day, a children's book about the life of an adopted Mandarin girl made its way into her hands while she was shopping for a gift. The book was the "sweetest children's book she had ever seen" she said, and recounting the story brought tears to her eyes. She took it home to show her husband, and the two started thinking seriously about what their life would look like with an adopted daughter.

Soon the day came for their IVF protocol. With as much preparation as she had put into balancing her hormones and strengthening her body, I figured (as did she) that it would work. Two attempts at IVF for this very healthy, now thirty-five-year-old woman resulted in no pregnancies.

However, their interest in adoption grew stronger all the time. I was thrilled to hear they had already started filing the application for the long process. What was most exciting was that Kristen's connection to her own sisters and the Mind-Body sisters inspired her and Jay to apply to adopt twin sisters from China, to have more than one child.

Both of them changed significantly after they made this decision and completed all of the steps involved in adoption. They became happier. They were freed, in a sense, at peace with themselves and excited to attempt this part of their journey together. They were able to participate in family and baby-centric events once again, contributing all the feelings of love they had previously buried down deep from suffering so many disappointments. Each day they felt anticipation, trusting they would soon have a family of their own.

In the end, their plan of adopting twin girls did not come to pass. The Universe instead gave them a Caucasian newborn baby girl who bears an uncanny resemblance to the two of them. Anyone receiving a family

Christmas card, unaware baby Kylee was adopted, would have little way of knowing this child was not biologically theirs. One might say the spirit of this baby was drawn to the overflowing amount of love coming from these two people whose hearts were broken open.

Chapter 33
Prepare for A Breakthrough

Somewhere near the end of her course of acupuncture treatments for fertility, a Well Women patient will come in presenting with what we call "The Readiness Factor." There is a certain new confidence about her. An almost tangible feeling of surrender surrounds her, indicating she has completely released her attachment to the fertility journey *outcome* and as a result, she is ready to mother a child. She has made profound internal and external changes, which have smoothed the path toward motherhood.

We believe this positive change is partially due to us constantly "sticking it" to them in the form of acupuncture treatments, spiritual truths, and recommended out-of-the-ordinary lifestyle suggestions that arouse their curiosity. However we look at it, *readiness is readiness*. It happens only when a woman is truly resolved with her process of infertility — emotionally, physically and spiritually. It can take months or years to become prepared for the parenthood adventure, and these women have learned that no amount of forcing makes babies arrive any sooner than they are scheduled.

This readiness, this level of preparation, cannot be faked. It produces a noticeable glow, similar to what resonates from people when they are in love. Women who cultivate this readiness factor in their lives do so by falling in love with their current life *as it is*.

Possibly years of fertility treatments have been reframed as something that has been going on during this time in their lives. The time no longer warrants being defined as a torturous process. There is peace. There is finally freedom from the "Why are we being punished?" thoughts.

Over the course of treatment, we spend hours sitting across from women in these acupuncture rooms, having a chance to reflect on which patterns have kept them stuck. Compassionately, we demonstrate the ways in which being afraid, holding on, not trusting, having a negative outlook, and being impatient have blocked them from becoming mothers. Likewise, eating harmful foods, insisting the baby arrive on their terms, or refusing to appreciate the life they already have are all sabotaging behaviors that do not serve them well.

In each acupuncture session we provide an awareness of these patterns and illuminate the opportunity for women to consciously redirect their energy in a healthier, more productive direction.

For women doing IVF, readiness is most often revealed at the time of their embryo transfer, the natural culmination point of the protocol. I have found acupuncture at the time of embryo transfer to be a key time to insert some spiritual awareness into this high-tech science.

During an IVF protocol, women stimulate their ovaries with hormone injections, then doctors surgically extract the resulting crop of eggs and fertilize them with sperm. Once fertilization occurs, the embryo cells divide in a petri dish. The potential exists for any embryo that continues dividing on days three or five of this process to be implanted into the woman and become new life. To have the embryos transferred back into the intended mother is a fascinating culmination point in the whole process. I have had the honor of attending hundreds of transfers to provide acupuncture, because it has been proven to help increase the chance of success.

When I am with my patients in this part of the process, on this important day, inside these transfer rooms at the various fertility clinics, I try to help the women see the magnitude of the work they have done. They have moved through the concepts explored in this book. At the time of the embryo transfer, I help them remember that they are ready for their lives to change; they have the option of realizing they are, indeed, ready for a new outcome. Women often report feeling liberated from the sadness of previous losses, receptive to the newly fertilized embryos, and peaceful in knowing they did their part to the best of their abilities. As a result, there is surrender, and that *is fertile.*

We cannot predict when or if readiness will happen for our patients; the journey sometimes seems to involve one step forward and two steps back. Watching a patient find peace within this process enough to subsequently surrender to a divinely orchestrated "master plan" is what makes the journey worth it for me as an observer and part of her team. Hearing of a positive pregnancy test two weeks later is wonderful, but it pales in comparison to the satisfaction that comes from seeing a woman decide to fully embrace her life, regardless.

Ready to Let Baby Walk Away

Having treated infertile patients for nearly fifteen years now, sometimes treating over sixty patients per week, I have seen more than my share of frustrated, disappointed women. Yet, my job never seems to get boring. Just when I think I have seen it all, a new woman appears who reveals to me that this spiritually based professional journey will never cease to inspire me. The reverence I have for this field goes far beyond the science involved in getting these children here.

In 2010 after I became pregnant with my second "against the odds" child, I gathered my repository of wisdom and inspirational stories collected over the years and blended that with the concept of "Cultivating a Fertile Garden" to create a live workshop named "Seed." It was originally a class I hosted in the lobby of California Fertility Partners (CFP) that intended to teach women about the *potential* that exists for fertility patients who were willing to learn about "Fertile Thoughts and Fertile Foods." It was such a success I created an online course to spread the wisdom across the globe (www.seedfertility.com).

Dr. Guy Ringler was instrumental in the creation of this program and its success. Later, both he and Dr. Kelly Baek endorsed the program to support the online version of the course, and mandated that brochures for the course be inserted inside the new patient folders for patients of CFP. Understanding the spiritual aspect of this program, Dr. Ringler referred a young woman named Jennifer to the Seed Program and suggested she meet with me for a dose of my own personal insight, as she prepared to do another round of IVF in the coming months.

Jennifer was only thirty-four, but she had lost a pregnancy at twenty-four weeks. She was telling herself the story that she would not be able to get beyond the loss of her son "Luke" sufficiently to get to another baby. In hopes of moving beyond this pain of loss, Jennifer signed up for the online version of my Seed course immediately.

Jennifer and her husband, Mike, had bicoastal homes to support their international social media marketing business, and the next time Jennifer was in Los Angeles, she booked an appointment with me in person to discuss what she was learning in my online course.

I was excited to meet with her and hear how well she was responding to this program I had spent four years putting together.

She said she was surprised by how much she was learning from the online course. The journaling questions were very poignant and led her exactly to the feelings that were bothering her so much. The biggest obstacle was clearly the loss of her son and the worry of how it would feel to say goodbye to him, to allow another child to come into her heart.

"Don't ask me to say goodbye to him, because he was my boy. I loved him. Though I never knew him, he was my son. I cannot say goodbye."

We talked for a few minutes about the difference between saying goodbye to a person and saying goodbye to the *pain* of losing a person. This smart woman understood and sighed deeply. Then she told me she continued to hear the word "footprints" in her head during quiet moments.

"Perhaps," I started, "you could buy a necklace charm of two footprints. It shouldn't be too hard to find. When you see the charm, imagine those footprints represent the time that you carried Luke in your belly, but now he walks his own path. When you see those footprints, you can imagine him walking away, being released as a free spirit."

With this, she burst into tears. Clearly, I had hit the right chord for her trapped feelings that needed expressing. She was ready to release Luke and free herself from the pain that persisted.

We followed the conversation with acupuncture. She went back to Florida and continued with the Seed program online course.

A few weeks later, she sent me an email prior to our scheduled "Seed Session" (a phone session intended to individualize the material from the online course) titled, "Please open before our phone call."

Intrigued, I opened the email to see a photo of a slate rock wall that had crumbled and two copper landscaping footprints on the ground in front of the rock debris.

When we talked on the phone she let me know many things had changed since her visit with me. She said when she returned to Florida she immediately began her search for footprints. At a nursery she found a pair of large landscaping feet and decided those were perfect to place on her property to symbolize Luke moving on.

What she had not anticipated was, within twenty-four hours of placing the feet next to the slate rock wall — stating out loud she was truly ready to release him, that the rocks would all fall to the ground!

Never had I witnessed a more obvious, outward sign of a "breakthrough." This little one communicated he was breaking free from the pain that kept them connected.

I have seen some amazing things happen for the women who have been patients of the Well Women office, and I have had some cool transformative, "paranormal" experiences, myself. But this was by far the most validating example of what is possible for women who are ready to heal and let go in order to reach their intended babies.

We acknowledged during that phone call her destiny had been forever changed as a result of this event.

One month later I heard from Jennifer again. Not only did their adoption proceedings finalize such that they were expecting a newborn in a few weeks, but also she was also a few weeks pregnant naturally!

This story suggests sometimes what we consider our time of greatest sorrow is the time when life is mysteriously preparing us; unknowingly helping us ready for what comes next.

Epilogue: My Own "Spirit Babies"

Throughout the course of this book I have illustrated what is possible when intuition and commitment to self-discovery blend with ancient wisdom, intention setting, diet changes, and a calm mind. It is the merging of all of these attributes that help women get to their children "against the odds."

When I reflect on how I personally overcame the challenges infertility presented me over and over again, I take my mind all the way back to 1997, when I was only twenty-seven, and a student of acupuncture who had never given much thought to my fertility. However, it was then I got my first clue that something interesting was planned for me in this lifetime.

That was the year I was finally off all the pharmaceuticals. I had returned to a healthy weight and was exercising. I had strengthened my body with Qi Gong that I learned in acupuncture school. And I was in a new relationship with a kind fisherman named Dan, whom I met at work before leaving my previous career in molecular biology.

I had never dated someone whose eyes stirred a feeling in me of a possible lifetime already spent together. When I looked into his eyes, I felt safe, even though we had frequent arguments about his ex-wife and my list of unmet expectations. The relationship was wildly co-dependent and rooted in our polar differences, nonetheless, we shared one common characteristic: the ability to "see" things intuitively.

I was in acupuncture school then, and was learning how to cultivate an above-average sensitivity in my fingertips, sculpting my intuitive muscles for future patients, and expanding my innate awareness. In the second year of school I took a few elective courses to develop my sixth sense, and

I received the attunement or initiation into a lineage of Reiki masters. My intuition was becoming quite strong.

Dan indulged me in conversations about extrasensory perception but admitted he had little interest in cultivating his own "psychic powers."

One weekend in early 1997, we traveled to central California to see his family. As I recall, we were staying in his mother's bedroom in the back of her large house. I remember the two of us hugging and kissing before getting ready for dinner. No one was home, but strangely I felt a strong "presence" in the far left corner of the room.

Was it a spirit hanging out in this older home? I asked Dan, "Do you feel that? It's like there's someone here with us. It feels like a little girl...over there, in the corner. It feels like something is *watching* us."

Dan surprised me. Normally he disregarded my paranormal musings, which drove me crazy. But this time he said, "Yes."

Shocked, I replied, "It's like she's evaluating us—like she wants to come to us, but I'm not having any kids! I'm in school, you have your daughter already, and I don't want kids now. How strange. Come on, let's finish getting ready for dinner. I don't want to give it any energy, whatever it is."

As time passed, my coursework demands intensified and the relationship crashed and burned, several times over. I never gave that afternoon a second thought.

Though we broke up, Dan was the first and only person I contacted when I got the news about my fertility. Something inside me said he would help if I called him, and I listened to that voice. After we agreed it was best not to have children if I intended to raise them on my own, I thought that was the end of it.

A few years later, what I believe was the "spirit" of that little girl started appearing in my office. One day, as I was cleaning one of my treatment rooms, I distinctly heard an authoritative voice say, "I am Kira Connors, and *I am coming to you.*"

I stopped in my tracks. Not because I was scared, but because I was intrigued. Had I imagined this? Had I been working too many hours? Why would a spirit want to come to me together with Dan Connors? I couldn't figure it to make any sense. I was in another relationship at the time that had not gone south yet, so I found this voice very confusing.

Another few years passed. Every so often, I would hear this voice delivering this same message. It increased in frequency and, I believe, started giving me more information. The message seemed to convey that *everything would be fine.* I sensed I was being presented with an opportunity to trust this inner voice, whomever it belonged to, as well as the opportunity to marvel at the natural unfolding of life's spiritual mysteries.

After another relationship ended, I gave in to this voice and attempted to find Dan. He had changed his phone number, address, and email. Having absolutely nothing in common, we had no mutual friends. These were the days before Facebook!

Truth be told, I really was not interested in rebooting that old relationship. I was content to keep searching for someone more "ideal" for me.

When the next encounter with "Kira Connors" occurred, I matter-of-factly told her (in my mind) *she* would have to orchestrate this happening between the two of us. She would have to put things in motion and have *him find me.* I would not force this issue where he was concerned. I relayed inwardly that I was now fully trusting in a "master plan" that would help me easily and effortlessly have my own child. To chase down an ex-boyfriend would suggest I did not trust that plan to come into being. After all, I now possessed the knowledge that I was the embodiment of the egg, and *she* always waits patiently!

Merely days after conveying my message to this little spirit, I received a call from Dan. More than four years had passed since we had spoken last, back when I previously asked him for sperm.

He said he found me on the web, looking to make amends with me for some old disappointments. He explained that weeks earlier he had lost his best friend, John, in a car accident that also took the lives of John's wife and three children, and that *an inner voice had told him to call me.*

"Did you have kids?" he asked.

"No, that hasn't worked out for me. But," I confided, "there is this little voice I hear when I'm in my office. She says she's Kira *Connors.*"

"Maybe we should have lunch and talk about that," Dan said. I agreed.

We met the next day. We talked for a long while, acknowledging that we were two very independent spirits, but agreed family life offered some nice rewards. Nearly ten years had passed since we felt that little girl's energy at his mother's house, yet now, at this time, it seemed we were ready and mature enough to consider creating a family together.

Our agreement was to try for six months naturally, and if it didn't happen we would part as friends. I would consider Kira's voice a random fantasy I imagined in an attempt to feel better while working with infertile patients.

At the start of the next cycle I checked my FSH. It was 15.6. Instead of panicking, I thought, "Hmm, that is interesting." Three weeks later, however, I was pregnant—with Kira Connors, who arrived when I was thirty-seven-years old. After all the suggestions to the contrary, I became pregnant effortlessly and naturally, five years after doctors told me I was in Premature Ovarian Failure and needed donor eggs.

Maybe some would say I fabricated that voice, using it as a coping mechanism to get past the potentially huge disappointment of not being able to have my own child. But that possibility never occurred to me. Her voice seemed real and it got my attention. I had dozens of other premonitory messages validated in my work with patients, so I was able to easily accept it as truth.

Kira's first year was not at all the "happily ever after" I had dreamed of. Instead, it was a year I had to focus on helping my terminally ill mother make it through her final days. It was a year full of emotional landmines to navigate. As I changed Kira's diapers and taught her how to walk, I helped my mother die with dignity, changing her when necessary, and carrying her when she could not take steps on her own.

In her final days, my mother asked what I planned to do with the rest of my life. What did I want, she asked, just in case she became "an angel able to help me from heaven above"?

"I would like to have a son, and I want more than anything to deliver my women's empowerment message to the world, instead of just helping the women individually who come to the office."

"Consider it done," she said, and passed peacefully a few days later.

I knew the stress of helping her pass had affected my ovaries. Out of curiosity, I checked my FSH soon after she died to see just how high it was. My score was almost 19 points! Statistically speaking, at age thirty-nine with an elevated FSH score and my history of severe endometriosis and blocked tube, there was about a 1% chance of conception, and likely it would end as a nonviable pregnancy due to advanced maternal age and mutated chromosomes.

Three months after my mother's transition, however, our son was conceived. Like Kira, Jack also was conceived with Dan, after one natural attempt only.

An early pregnancy ultrasound revealed Jack's egg had ovulated from my right ovary and traveled successfully through the previously "blocked" fallopian tube! He arrived weeks before my fortieth birthday, weighing a solid eight-and-one-half pounds, defying all the odds stacked against him.

My ability to give birth to Kira and Jack strongly suggests that life, with its myriad of frustrations and disappointments, will test us repeatedly *to stay open and trusting that life is working for our good.* The more we can make peace with this spiritual truth, the more we can attract the things we want most out of life.

My claim to hear, sense, and visualize Kira Connors is an example of the phenomena of "Spirit Babies"—described in the book with the same title by Walter Makichen. He explains that little ones hover above us before choosing when to arrive. These unborn spirits decide when to come, to whom, and under what conditions. My son Jack surprised us at age four, when he announced out of nowhere during dinner one evening, that he decided to come to our family when he "saw Kira inside Mommy's tummy."

While life certainly has stuck it to me many times, and in so many painful ways, I would go back and repeat everything exactly the same way if it meant getting to these two amazing souls who arrived under these interesting conditions. Wayne Dyer's final book, *Memories of Heaven,* expands on this idea; he presents a collection of stories children reveal of their time in a spirit form, prior to coming to earth to be with their families.

When I ask Dan, now a dear friend and my co-parenting partner in this journey, if he regrets having kids with me in such an unconventional setting (as unmarried friends living together platonically) he says, "Are you kidding? A world without Kira and Jack just wouldn't be right."

There's a reason so many of us are being asked to take the pokes infertility sticks to us, insisting we raise our vibration and be our best selves. From what I have seen, fertility challenges appear to be necessary preparation for us to be ready and able to raise children who are very different than we were as kids, and who are much more evolved than any prior generation.

This new generation (also known as "Indigo Kids" or "Crystal Children" to those in the spiritual community) appears to be more confident, intuitive, self-aware, and hard wired to heal and change the world with their contributions. This certainly holds true for the children I know who have been born to my dedicated patients, and my own children, as well.

As you absorb the concepts in this book, consider (or trust) that your cellular processes have potentially been "activated" and changed for the better from reading these pages. The women in this book turned their fertility challenges into children, and they improved their lives in the process.

The same chance exists for you to begin reframing all the sticks and jabs in life, turning the heartbreaks into a sublime beauty and wisdom that will define this chapter of your life. Each challenge or disappointment provides an opportunity for you to look inside and make the adjustments necessary to nurture your baby, and yourself. The next time infertility metaphorically sticks it to you; stick it back—with wisdom, understanding and grace.

In Conclusion...

These true stories reveal what is possible for the many women who begin making different choices with respect to how they view their infertility. Despite their best efforts to embody these concepts and change their mindset, unfortunately there will still be women destined to remain childless. Welcoming the "presence of Spirit" into their lives, or making an attempt to embrace a spiritual attitude about life, is highly recommended for these women - so they may come to know a different sense of fulfillment in their lives.

While my life now includes the joy of mothering two children, it began changing to include more joy long before they arrived. As I accepted that mine is a life of service, centered around teaching women how to embrace the spiritual transformation that lies waiting for them within the context of infertility, I finally discovered the sense of contentment I never realized had been waiting there for me all along.

Kira and Jack are thriving little beings who came into existence due to the shifts I made in my life to prepare for their arrival. They represent what is possible when we say YES! to our destiny.

ACKNOWLEDGEMENTS

My women's empowerment message would not have the same healing impact if it were not for the huge contributions made by acupuncturist, herbalist, and wise woman Anna Werderitsch, my "twin flame." She is the co-creator of the Well Women Acupuncture vision and philosophy. Working together, we pioneered a new approach to an ancient medicine, creating a unique style of acupuncture that is geared to the emotional and spiritual needs of the modern Western woman.

By *living* the concepts outlined in this book, we empowered ourselves, our patients, and hope to inspire women everywhere. Anna, I can never thank you enough for helping me shed the layers of negativity that kept me stuck. Your wisdom, love, and supportive friendship is truly what made pregnancy and motherhood possible for me.

The courageous and graceful Well Women Acupuncture *patients* are to receive all the credit for any inspiration derived from these stories. They put their faith in me, trusted me with their hearts (and second hearts), and that has transformed me into an extraordinary practitioner and a Well Woman. Working with these amazing women every day provides me the constant passion and inspiration necessary to put these ideas about reframing infertility into the world. I am grateful to every woman who has walked through my office door, for I still believe I learn something precious in each interaction.

My mother, Betty Thornberry, was a single mother who instilled in me the spiritual belief that *an opportunity always lies somewhere inside disappointment*—the very essence of this book. She now resides as a spirit in a peaceful space far beyond life's disappointments, and continues to inspire me on a daily basis.

Certain talented individuals played a prominent role in the early preparation for my life's work ~ particularly Debi Frankle, MFCC, and acupuncturist David Wells. I will never be able to thank them enough for the positive impact they each had on my physical and emotional health, and personal transformation.

Immense gratitude goes to the visionaries along my path—Daoshing Ni, Bob Flaws, John James, Russell Friedman, Carolyn Myss, Christiane Northrup, Alison Armstrong, and Michael Bernard Beckwith. Each of these insightful individuals provided me with glimpses of the spiritual framework necessary for me to help troubled hearts.

Visionary author Michael Crichton and his wife Sheri deserve special acknowledgement for motivating me to complete this work in 2007. Though Michael passed way before his time and is not here to see the book come to life, I appreciate that he saw enough merit to this book to offer to help me get it published.

Dozens of medical doctors in Los Angeles have facilitated the growth and credibility of the Well Women Acupuncture office, providing a steady stream of referrals. These doctors recognize that our emotions play a very strong role in healing. "Thank you" goes especially to the late Dr. Joyce Vargyas, Dr. Richard Marrs, Dr. Guy Ringler, and Dr. Kelly Baek of California Fertility Partners. Their continued support of this unique approach to treating infertility has helped bridge the gap between Eastern and Western medicine, and the number of women who benefit continues to grow every day.

My closest friends and office colleagues have maintained an interest in this book and awaited its arrival for years now. I appreciate their patience and encouragement throughout the book's gestation and birthing process. Particular thanks goes to Jennifer Block for her help with editing and for cheering me on when needed. To Francine Graff, I am thankful for so many wonderful things, most especially the insight passed on to me in 2003; our time spent together truly changed my life forever. Patty Gonzalez, a "Latina Buddha" who always knows when I need encouragement along this path, deserves special recognition and gratitude, as well. Sarah McCune Morgan, whose friendship is felt across the miles and spans many lifetimes, has been like a sister to me. A special thank you is reserved for Tamara Gould, for her insightful input along this long journey. Jess McNeil-Estes shared her artistic brilliance to create the book's cover.

My "spiritual stepdaughter" Kaitlyn Connors deserves a distinct acknowledgment for reminding me to "Let life happen." Thank you, Kaitlyn, for your wisdom, your friendship, and for loving KJ with all of your heart.

I am especially grateful to Ananda Edmonds, who trusted her intuitive voice enough to introduce me to eloquent writer Kuwana Haulsey, who found the time in her busy life to participate in this work.

I am so grateful to my brother Chad, who has always been supportive of my unique path. No matter how different our journeys have been and how far apart they may take us, he continues to support all of my dreams. My father, Jerry Thornberry showed up when I needed him the most, and I will always love him for that.

I thank Michael Smith for providing endless emotional support and loving friendship while I follow my personal dreams.

Dan Connors deserves a special thank you, because he gave me the two gifts I treasure most in life, and continues to participate in this amazing adventure with me, never knowing what will happen next.

Lastly, I am so grateful to Kira and Jack Connors for being able to understand how important it is that I share their inspirational stories. I thank the two of them for completely changing the course of my life, and in the process, the lives of all the women I work with.

Printed in the United States
by Baker & Taylor Publisher Services